HOW TO LIVE WITH YOURSELF

How To Live
With Yourself

DAVID SEABURY

SCIENCE OF MIND PUBLICATIONS
Los Angeles, California

Fourth Printing - August 1984

Published by SCIENCE OF MIND PUBLICATIONS
3251 West Sixth Street, Los Angeles, California 90020

ISBN 0-911336-39-7

CONTENTS

FOREWORD

Living would become much easier if we discovered our emotional inadequacies and corrected them. For the most part we do not realize in what ways our lives are distorted.

Basically, everyone, in one respect or another, is neurotic. The only person who is not unbalanced in some manner is the individual who does not have the intelligence to disrupt his life, namely a moron.

So be glad you are normal and do have problems, although you may not admit it. In this book David Seabury points out the many subtle ways you may misdirect your basic emotions, thus depriving yourself of a fuller, more joyous experience of living.

Not only does he spell out the nature of some of your hidden difficulties, but he gives concrete and specific directions for eliminating them so that you can become a greater expression of the Life that flows in and through you.

For more than forty years Dr. Seabury was the great exponent of the new psychology, which had a spiritual foundation, and he was a famed national figure.

This is the fifth volume of his works which has been published posthumously. The previous titles are: *Stop Being Afraid, Release from Your Problems, Pull Yourself Together, Heaven, Hell, and Happiness, and Your Four Great Emotions.*

Science of Mind Publications

CHAPTER I

EMOTIONS GOVERN YOUR LIFE

Many years ago, in the early days of my lecturing throughout the United States, I was asked during the question period of one of the lectures, "Is there any kind of person who would be apt to be free of neurosis?"

With perhaps too little thought of the possible shock I might produce in my audience, I said, "Well, the only example I can think of at the moment is a moron. It takes intelligence and sensitivity to become neurotic."

I then advised my listeners not to be disturbed if they discovered they were neurotic. I assured them it was more a sign of endowment than a disgrace; in fact, that it generally indicated more than usual possibilities. And were it worth anyone's time and labor, statistics might be gathered to prove that the degree of a neurotic habituation corresponds mathematically with the degree of intelligence and general awareness of life and its great potentiality.

You can't condition nothing, and the more facets a personality has, the greater is the possibility of their producing confusion in him from the crosscurrents of his early experience.

This of course does not mean that every intelligent and sensitive person is pushed into a wholly neurotic outlook on life. If an infant has the good fortune to be raised by wise, loving, and reasonably patient parents, he may escape many of the influences that bring on neurosis. But the demands of life are extensive, and parents themselves struggle with emotional pressures. So the need for deeper understanding of the intricate reactions of human beings upon each other — the whats, hows, and whys of the progress of life on Earth — has become more than ordinarily important.

In other words, we need to show people how to handle the discomforts of neurosis, and little by little reduce them down to less and less of a nuisance. For neurosis is not a comfortable condition. Nevertheless, its unease can be reduced by becoming more effectively acquainted with the everyday rules and ruses of the human mind, and, even more importantly, with the nature of emotion. For its persistant power is the toughest factor we humans have to handle in setting our sights on a civilization that can remain permanent.

Another plain fact that has not been clarified enough for the person suffering from the distortions of emotion is that *he is not his neurosis*. It is a collection of misconceptions about himself and life that he has taken on, which are dragging hard against the development of his ease and confidence in living. These peculiarities do not fairly represent his nature; they represent the conditioning of his nature. Most of all they indicate the twisted responses of his variety and force of feeling.

Not All Conditioning Is Harmful

Yet the influence of conditioning can be wholesome and helpful. So it devolves upon education to see to it that the training of young children, from birth to leaving school, becomes closer and closer to the best we know and can learn about handling our own natures. Thus child training can be good as well as bad. But a kind of brainwashing does go on that clouds many a child's concept of himself, and thus affects his handling of experience. He becomes conditioned to twisted or half-true concepts and unruly habits of mind that lead him away from attaining a practice of life that makes him a safe and sane citizen of the world.

And, if our training has lacked understanding of sensible concepts, we very much need to be assured that deep within us all the usual elements of our unconditioned nature are still there, and can be reclaimed. If these character factors have not been too seriously affected, we ourselves can return them to their normal nature, provided we will learn what is needed and act upon it.

So, essentially, what is neurosis?

From one very important standpoint neurosis is merely the effect upon us of our own ignorance and that of other people. If this is so, our contention that this mental-emotional unease, neurosis, is no disgrace, is correct. For we are born in a state of ignorance, and cannot be blamed for that fact. We have had to find out in rather a painful way that learning is our one chance of survival and development. And it is increasingly so as more and more individuals arrive on this planet, each with his own automatic urge to have and to hold what he or she desires.

But we should keep in mind that this condition, which has seemingly suddenly appeared in our midst and been named neurosis, is the result of nothing more than our old bugbear, ignorance, and should not be blown up into a new scarehead merely because it is called by a new name. We should beware of the unwise human habit of enlarging the problems brought on by ignorance into giant-sized symbols of doom. Ignorance can melt in a minute when knowledge and calm attention are applied to it.

True, ignorance is a kind of doom, and must be persistently reduced as fast as we are able to do it. And we must admit that there is one aspect of neuroses that increases the job of understanding how to deal with them. That aspect is the fact that they do not function in the visible world of matter, but in the still evasive world of thought and feeling. And this is why, though we justly have an excited reverence for science, we must calmly realize that its tenets, awe-inspiring as they are, are quite possibly inadequate to deal with data related to hate and love, fury and generosity, lust and self-command, inquisitiveness but privacy for others.

The Scientist's Bedrock Attitude

However, the scientist's attitude, which is the bedrock of his success, applies as well to the psychology of human nature as to the relationships in the physical world. In other words, he seeks truth by using controlled attention. He sees that submitting the personal ego to the pursuance of such truth is the means by which the secrets of the cosmos can be known, and its pleasures and protections enjoyed. Of course, persuading the ego to admit to mastership other than its own is not easy to attain.

But we cannot afford to favor science for its remarkable discoveries and their application over and above the very center of importance in life for all of us. And that unquestionably is the well-being of mankind itself, which is incontrovertably tied to the power of emotion and its bondage in neurosis. Solving this demand, that man's gaining command over his enormously powerful emotions be given first place as an agenda on the list of life's needs, can hardly be overlooked.

An attitude of know-it-all destroys the value of any curative process. In fact, unless we are able to recognize the naivete of the subconscious, we will continue to shut ourselves off from therapeutic help. For emotional therapeusis is not an intellectual process. Its success rests upon the longing to be adjusted to life so that one can know joy.

"There is one thing you psychologists do that makes me very angry," a brilliant lawyer told me. "You may say all you like about the importance of emotion, along with thought, in accomplishing the cure of neurotic states, but why do you ask me to stop using my wits?"

"We don't," I protested. "We ask you to use them more accurately and concern yourself with more primary values than those you ordinarily use."

"But you expect me to become subjective and dreamy, pretty nearly going to sleep when using your methods," he said angrily.

"Yes, that's right," I agreed. "We would like to have a person do his work in much the mood he is when sitting gazing into an open fire, or while musing in bed at night."

"But that's what I resist," he pursued. "Why can't I be on my toes intellectually: critical, keen, skeptical of all that is being considered?"

"Because changes of consciousness never develop that way. Criticism is a kind of hate. It disagrees. You cannot hate yourself out of ill health. You must believe yourself into a cure. Give the method your 'accepting' attention, even give it a fair try before just running it down. Did you ever have an inspiration?" I added.

"Sure," he said. "The best of my legal work depends on what I call flashes," the lawyer suddenly admitted.

"And did you ever stop to edit critically what you were thinking, to get it perfect?"

"Yes, I've done that."

"Well, what happened?"

The legal eyes regarded me quizzically. "Well, I found I couldn't get my inspiration back."

"Exactly. It's that way with therapeutic work. An inspiration comes from the creative level of the mind, the level which must be reached if psychological changes are to take place. You can't contact that level if you are being critically editorial, so you can't get any constructive impressions *into* that level if you're argumentative about it. Dr. Samuel Johnson wrote: 'I am willing to love all mankind except an American.' That was an emotionalized prejudice, wasn't it?''

"I should hope so," my companion laughed.

"Now, if a man had any such biased attitude, do you think an intellectual discussion would have changed him?"

"No. I've spent too many years in the law to believe that."

"Well, neither can a man be brought out of the emotionalized fixations of neurosis by intellectual discussion. He must be willing to let therapeutic exercises and the reading of sensible psychological books be an experience to which he exposes himself in the way he reaches for inspiration in his work. Otherwise, he only stuffs his head full of facts, and still has all his emotional fixations. He may trick others by a pseudo open-mindedness, but he can't trick himself. The reactions of the subconscious are law-abiding. By which I mean they respond automatically to a universal condition — the law that a given stimulus invokes a given response. The pattern of the stimulus and the response are unique for the individual, but the 'soul' — the essence of it — is universal."

Don't Be Embarrassed by Neurosis

We are continually asked if everyone can be helped out of neurosis, and the answer is, "No, not unless the person frees his conscious mind of those barriers which stand in the way of reaching the obsessing difficulties in the subconscious depths." This is why we make the point of not being embarrassed over having some neurotic habits. Being ashamed of it will summon pride quicker than a flash, and for the time cut off completely the adult intelligence that would be perfectly willing to admit the problem.

The main thing we need in freeing ourselves from the disadvantages of neurotic habits is a belief that learning is as important as physical food. Indeed it is a food, for it makes the mind grow as food sustains and renews the body. We cannot afford to stop adding to our knowledge, and we do need to bring understanding of the outer, objective world and the inner world of meaning into better balance. We cannot leave either one of these "facts of life" out of our search for answers and attain a full, safe, and satisfying existence. We should extend our respect for meaning, and be somewhat less avid about acquiring facts without applying meanings to them from that invisible world which thought and emotion motivate.

I would like to see people well, successful, and at peace. I believe they can move continually toward that goal if they can bring themselves to believe that they are more affected by their own thought, and compelled by the force of their emotions, than they are by any physical or objective conditions of their lives.

We do have physical bodies, but these apparently so significant bodies of ours are helpless instruments in the power of the mighty invisibility — emotion. Fortunately for us they have aids and assistants to help out, like judgment, imagination, and desire. But the greatest of these is desire.

There is a serious problem, however, in presenting therapeutic methods to sophisticated readers. We have learned that the more efficient the process, the more childish it may seem to intellectually critical people. They forget that we were children when we became neurotic, and are children still in approaching its cure. They forget also that as morbid mental states are essentially irrational, they can only be influenced by methods sufficiently consistent to reach their own level. In fact, because of the emotional nature of neurosis, there often seems to be an absence of logical rationality in the ways by which it is cured.

We feel that our adult attitudes ought to be used, but the actual fact is they are not as powerful as the emotion bottled up in the neurosis, and that must be admitted and the misunderstandings of youth drained off before an individual's intelligence can reach the source of the problem. Nor does his attention have much chance of serving intelligence until he has allowed the fierce emotion to be drained away by a sharper understanding of what this tremendous system of urges means in and to experience.

The Folly of Wanting the Impossible

Allegory and folklore are saturated with proof of the instinctive awareness we have of the errors of judgment we all make. For instance, what is the hint contained in the folk phrase, "He wants to eat his cake and have it too"? We know it is a hidden reference to greed, and that it pictures asking for an impossibility. But many of us go on harboring such desires, and subconsciously rebel against the impossibility of their being fulfilled.

The development of a better handling of our lives is often delayed by this incredible determination to have what is impossible. There is no provision in the great aggregate of natural laws that permits us to eat a piece of cake and yet have it to eat all over again. Another piece, yes, or the same type of ingredients in a different form, but not that same piece of cake.

A certain degree of limitation has to exist in life or we would be deprived of many, many conveniences and enjoyments. You cannot have a glass of water without a glass. You cannot quench your thirst with sea water. You cannot prevent water from turning into steam if it is subjected to heat.

Life is one great mass of laws, weaving in and out of relationship to each other, and producing the incredible patterns of matter and consciousness for our use and delight. But yes, there is a catch! If we do not become willing to learn these laws in all their forms, and acknowledge the Creator who conceived their interaction, pandemonium is possible.

Neurosis is as common as the common cold, and as uncomfortable to experience. Its degree and formation are mainly brought into being by the impact of a person's home setting upon the design of his or her nature. His day-by-day well-being is more acutely concerned with the form this disturbance takes than is usually understood. Every nature having its own design, within which emotion plays an immensely important part, what we could call emotional quantity and quality decide very specifically what an individual has to deal with in freeing himself from the clutch of neurosis.

As we have said, to become neurotic a person has to have a degree of intelligence and of sensitivity. If his reactions to experience — that is, his thought and emotions — are oversimplified, his reactions are not complex and give him little or no trouble. They do not "tangle" as do those of a person who has a greater range of emotional response.

So in finding out how to deal with this pestering leviathan, neurosis, we must face up to the truth that it is a common experience. It is a misadventure in the process of evolution, a misdirection on the road to full command of the incredible list of potential powers with which the Creator has endowed us. We are all exposed to unintelligent conditioning of one sort or another. We make a great pother about education, but mostly leave it delving into matters of material significance, allowing those of vital meaning to be pretty definitely demoted to a level where they become suspect of weakness or secondary merit.

In taking up the purpose of encouraging people to believe that they can do something to free themselves from the dragging weight of neurosis, we need then to emphasize the fact that it is nothing to be ashamed of. First of all, we must acknowledge that we are dealing with a subjective factor primarily. Its relation to our preoccupation with objective matters is more important than we seem to realize, but its ascendancy over objective existence is a truth we are wildly foolish to ignore. For if we do ignore it, we are very likely to pay with the loss of our ever-tempting objective rewards. If our subjective relation to life — our thinking and feeling processes — is allowed to be neglected, scorned, scoffed at, or radically ridiculed, we risk losing every chance for emotional serenity, and our pile-up of objects becomes of very little value to us.

Education's Most Productive Goal

Ability to discriminate among the vast number of values and meanings life holds can hardly be questioned as the most productive goal among all the goals education offers. Possession of money is not to be excluded as a goal, since it is a direct means to the advance of life. But if it is elevated too greatly among the gamut of goals life has to offer, it will destroy the central evolutionary goal, which is the release of the individual's creative ability. Money is a servant of life. It is fatal to make it king.

Balanced understanding is the goal that can offer the individual the greatest and most permanent satisfactions. Imbalance in any aspect of living tips the life process to the point where it has to be ceaselessly set straight, the process having to be started again and again, with the debit of much lost time and constant threat. We are coming to see that badly handled emotion is the perfect example of constantly tipping over the process of evolution. It most fearfully upsets the balance of emotional effects by leaving it with the scar tissue of such things as hate and desire for revenge. And that just throws the whole thing back from where it has to be started all over again. The only way hate can safely be used is against evil, not people.

Since neurosis is a fact of life in the present day, and is being presented from so many angles, many of which are complex, an effort to get at the common trends of this human unease would make it less difficult to deal with. Presenting complexities first and simplicities afterward is only too apt to leave a blur of uncertainty in the mind. Anything one wishes or needs to learn is better comprehended if the primary causes are explained before one becomes involved in the overwhelming details that develop from most great causes. Love and wisdom, and their use, are elemental causes of the life process and lead through phalanx after phalanx of reactions, comprehensions, constructions, estimations, arguments, reversals — on and on through the processes life is composed of. Just two causes and an avalanche of effects. It is obvious that knowing more about what is a cause and what is an effect is necessary to help us to know how to keep the power of choice from tangling itself into wasteful delays.

Nerves Are Messengers — Emotions Are Dynamos

We need to realize that neurosis is named in a way that turns our attention to the nervous system rather than to the emotional system, which is the main basis of its painful reactions. The nerves are messengers; the emotions are dynamos, activists. We should not give the nerves the attention that is due the emotions, lest we neglect getting command of the cause, emotion, and overemphasize the mere messengers, the nerves. In neurosis we are dealing with the primary emotions summoned by the nerves. Our emotions essentially govern our lives. It is they that prompt action. They set things going; otherwise we would remain mere observers, and there would in effect be no life.

In the end it is rage, fear, sex, and wonder that become neurotic. Nerves are the telephone system of the body, but emotion is the dynamic power of the human organism causing it to act: to produce life, as it were. Emotion represents the great "I-Want," another way of saying that it is the root reaction area of the life process. It decides whether we are to enjoy or be miserable, to succeed or fail, to worship or defame, to protect or destroy.

How well we are able and willing to direct our emotions into safe and sane action decides the whole quality of life — sane and enjoyable, or dangerous and unhappy. It appears that we cannot continue to handle these reactions so carelessly. We must admit the threat of their power when ungoverned, and set ourselves to diminish the threat so that we can discover how to gain the satisfying rewards of being alive.

A first requirement for anyone desiring to be rid of neurosis, then, is to have some understanding of the hazardous concepts and habits forced upon him by its influence. He can then clear his mind for action against this set of habits that is keeping the action of his intelligence captive in concepts formed in his childhood but largely inadequate to direct his adult life.

CHAPTER II

TAKE COMMAND OF YOUR EMOTIONS

Meeting the Emergency

During the earlier days of the First World War a young man came to see me. He was soon to leave for Europe to fill a demanding job with the United States military personnel. His special skills had put him in the position of having much to offer the war effort. But this man was badly conditioned emotionally. His secret doubts and fears were torturing him to a degree that threatened his stability on the job.

We talked, and from what he told me I mentally made a retrospective analysis of his life. There were several years in his experience, from the age of eight until around the middle of college, when he underwent a number of shocks. And these had set up inner pressures that flattened his self-confidence and frustrated him at every turn.

What to do?

He was leaving in a week. There was no time for normal analysis and therapy. Under the pressure of the need I invented a technique.

"You understand, don't you," I said to him, "that under the circumstances we can't follow the usual methods for helping you?"

His expression changed from interest to a kind of despair. "You mean you think it's hopeless . . . ?" I could see the evidence of the reflex of discouraged feeling that had so plagued his life.

"Now, wait," I urged him. "If you are really in earnest about wanting to get out of these troublesome reactions, and can put your adult intellect on the shelf temporarily, I can make a suggestion that could start the release from your condition."

There was a tentative smile on his face, but I saw the doubt and incredulity that were gathering in his mind. Before continuing I pinned down the meaning of what I saw in his reaction, and described it to him cold turkey. We were up against a matter of emergency and the desperation of his need.

"I'm willing to take time to describe the method that I want you to use, but I warn you that it will offend your intellect. I also warn you that if you expect your intellect to effect a cure you will be immensely disappointed. You are not your brain. It's only one part of your response pattern, although a mighty useful one. But it gave you very little help at the age you were first called upon to endure the experiences that distorted your relation to life. You were mostly 'feeling' at that time. In fact, you were floored by feeling. The intellect you have since released has had very little ability in coming to your aid."

"All right, all right," he said testily. "What do you want me to do?"

So I told him I wanted him to be his own analyst, to imagine himself as the dazed and frightened kid he had been when his worst conditioning began. "See that boy," I said. "Take him into bed with you at night and get him to talk to you, to tell you what it all felt like, what it did to you. Give him time to spill it all out. Don't for heaven's sake moralize about it. That, if it must, will come later. First in importance is permission to unload any rejection, any injustice or neglect. Let this image of your young self clear the air, so that he can start fresh and allow you a chance to help him resee the whole thing. Then use your intellect, your sympathies, your adult observation of life, and explain to the boy the meanings of what happened. Comfort the worst agonies, but go on to the need to let it all go, to refuse to allow it to keep interfering in your normal life."

He sat looking aghast, as though he regretted having gotten himself into quite such an odd fix.

"Come on," I said, "chuck your pride in the wastebasket and give that boy the help he needs."

He stood up and put out his hand uncertainly, looking like a man in shock. "Well," he said, unbelievingly, "I suppose I could try."

We shook hands, he still dazed and I wondering if he could get past his pride. It was asking a good deal as people go.

"You've got to be in earnest," I said seriously. "It won't work without that. And above all things, do not say one word to anyone else about what you are doing. I'm sorry to have to say it, but I very much doubt that you know anyone who 'could keep his hands off.' And however good his comments might be they would definitely break the flow of the process you had started and lead you into dangerous doubt. Give the whole thing up and wait for a chance at sound counseling rather than risk the effect on you of the uncontrolled expression of another person's ego. A person might be honestly anxious to help you, but through no fault of his own be quite incapable of avoiding the expression of his own opinion, which would be just as apt to hinder his effort to free you as to help you.

"What I am suggesting to you is an emergency method. It needs particular protections. If or when — I hope when — you feel you are really succeeding with the therapy, you can have companionship in the experiment. But first you must be sure it works. You must be confident enough of it to be able to defend it."

I saw him twice more before he left, and added something to the hints I had given him about how to proceed: "Reeducate your youthful self out of the resistance to your father's harshness and your mother's prudery. Get him to understand it and forgive them. You can't afford to give time to any desire to blame them. Remember, they were conditioned too. We all have been. There is always a way to understand anything, even if we have to resort to accepting other people's ignorance."

It was nearly a year before I saw the man again. A great deal must have happened, and a faithful effort had been made. He was infinitely more relaxed than he had been. His handshake was forceful enough to be almost crippling.

"You've done a good job," I told him, after he had given me a picture of the results he had obtained.

"You know," he said, "I didn't believe it." A grin spread over his face. "But I'm glad you did," he added, and wrung my hand again, painfully.

The Logic of Self-help

My interest in self-help was strengthened. Yes, I have seen too many help themselves to doubt what can be done, within sensible limits. But the important truth that everybody must ultimately "make a cure possible himself" was certainly substantially demonstrated. The logic of it is clear. We need to recognize that our lives lose interest if we allow them to get out of our own hands. We should not surrender the vitality of our own judgment about our right relation to life; not if we want to hang onto the basic vitality that keeps us alive, healthful, and interesting.

We take this need for "methods" pretty much for granted in our approach to things like making and running machines of all sorts, producing conveniences: furniture, automobiles, household helps, and the like. But we have dealt with emotion from a standpoint that did not create a clear or persuasive enough understanding to bring the necessary universal response. In other words, people respond to ideas and demands that they believe will pay; that is, make life safer, more enjoyable and rewarding. They will work for such things, for they know that accomplishment without action is impossible.

The chance of relief from neurotic trials, discomforts, and disappointments, then, is solidly based on self-help and self-knowledge, however much assistance we receive from experts. At least this is true in the realm of emotional experience, which is pretty much the basis of all our personal troubles.

As a matter of important fact, the cure of a nagging mental or emotional disturbance cannot be brought about without the agency of self-help. However excellent the therapy given, in the end it is the individual himself who must produce the cure. For no one can force him to cooperate and make the necessary effort to become well adjusted.

In the controversy that started when emotional counseling was a new idea, and at something of a disadvantage from lack of sufficient verification, the value of self-help was seriously questioned. It seemed to smack too much of possible ineptness or even danger. So an obvious factor in the dilemma was given scant attention: the simple truth that in the end the only possible way anyone can be assured of being helped out of neurotic problems is by self-help. Anything we wish to attain for ourselves in the realm of personal development must be attained by ourselves. No one else has the key to our real feelings. Actually we wouldn't want them to have, although we do long for and can well use assistance.

As to the question, Can one help oneself? it has happened too many times to doubt its possibilities. Also, one should say that much of the material dealing with practical psychology is useful for anyone, even though he may be relatively free of neurosis. Education of the emotions is even more important than learning to spell, valuable as that is, for if a person is ruled by out-of-control emotion, expertise in a well-spelled vocabulary could be pretty much beside the point. Parents need practical knowledge of the vagaries of emotion for their own freedom from personal distress, but also to save their children from duplicating such distress. Religion has tried to assist in the problem of taming this great energy embedded in the organism of human beings. But it made the mistake of attempting merely to stifle it, which would destroy the power and enthusiasm, the potential for productive interest and attainment, in the living of life.

One of the basic objectives of religion should be, it would seem, to elevate the value of emotion so that it became thoroughly understood that, rightly used, feeling could bring about the regeneration of human behavior, for feeling is the very fulcrum of human power. Misused, it threatens man's existence. Rightly handled, it has accomplished, by the force of desire, every great act and movement in the history of mankind.

No one would deny that for unusual human dilemmas and maladjustments specially trained technicians are needed. But it should not be true for troubles like self-consciousness, hypersensitivity, self-indulgence, self-pity, false guilt, average inferiority, and so on. People bothered by such common discomforts cannot all retire on sick leave. And it hardly seems that deep analysis, which costs so much in time and money, and sometimes results in added confusion, should be required to treat these ordinary emotional maladies.

A day will come when parents will know how to ward off much of this emotional reaction in a child's relation to early experience. They will have a capacity to read the play of emotion in a child as he meets life's demands, and provide the explanations that will show him how to resolve disturbing incidents at the time they occur. And this will do much to prevent such disturbances being buried in the subconscious in a distorted form. Experience for the young will then be more of a true education than a lottery in which everyone is apt to lose as much as he gains.

My Client Invents a Technique

Another experience I had with a client, in relation to the development of self-help techniques, comes to mind. The method was invented by the client himself, but I found it effective in other cases. It was another situation where a limitation produced the idea that solved the problem.

A gray-haired man sat in my office smiling from ear to ear. I hadn't seen him for several years, and then for only one hour. He hadn't spoken yet but his smile strongly suggested good humor and apparent contentment. I had remembered his expression when I last saw him as strained, anxious, almost bitter.

"I came to see you about three years ago," he began, set off by what must have been my astonished expression at the change in him. "I see you remember how I looked when I saw you last," he added.

"I do," I agreed. "What happened to you?"

"I told you I needed help badly but couldn't afford more than one session. You may remember you diagnosed my condition as primarily a persecution complex. I told you I'd always been hypersensitive. You wanted to know if I recalled getting my feelings hurt when I was six months old. I said that was ridiculous, of course. You said so was my idea that I was born hypersensitive — maybe sensitive, but not hypersensitive. We went over some of my early experiences, and you pointed out when it was that the sensitivity began to be hyper."

"I remember," I said. "Since you weren't able to come back again I suggested you could help yourself if you would go over those painful experiences from the standpoint of a mature man, see them fully, vividly, with all the emotion you felt at the time . . ."

"Then to detach them from my memory," he interrupted, "to drop them into limbo and resee everything from the standpoint of the way a grown man would see it."

"That's right," I admitted, "but you said you couldn't come again. I couldn't just leave you with nothing to help you out. All I could do was cast a hook . . . What happened? I see that something did."

"You hooked me," he said. "You tried so hard to help in that short time, it inspired me to see what I could do."

"So?"

He sat forward in a kind of triumph of success. "I invented a substitute for the counseling sessions."

"You what?" I said, startled and interested.

"I decided that if I could have afforded to see you, I'd have come an hour a day for at least three months. So I dated myself with your memory, just as I would have liked to have done with you."

"You arranged interviews with my memory?" I repeated, now ready for anything.

"Sure. It would have been necessary to leave my office early if I had come here every day at four o'clock. So I went home instead. I took up one of your books and read awhile. I thought back about things that had hurt me in the past. I reasoned out what you would have said to me . . . how you would have interpreted the situations. They began to seem a lot different after all the intervening time. I felt kind of foolish to be letting them make my temper and self-pity flare up. I began to see the absolute connection between those old feelings of being rejected and my depressions now. I just can't take them so seriously anymore."

He took a piece of paper from his pocket as he finished and glanced at it. Then he said with obvious satisfaction, "I had just one hundred and seventy-four interviews with you. Not bad, considering I only had to pay for one . . . er . . . two," he added, as he took out his wallet.

Our thoughts, all the time, are forming the quality — the success or failure, enjoyment or boredom — of our relation to experience. Thought molds us like putty. And if it were not for our incredibly valuable power to choose, and our quantum of spiritual discernment, we humans could become either kaleidoscopes of confused ineptitude or endless warring brutes.

Here and there some of us have done so.

The deepest reprieve there is in life is to be able to take expert command of our own emotions; to encourage their positive expression and forbid the negative. For they are loaded with misery and illness for those who look upon unbridled emotion as a prime factor of personal freedom; whereas freedom from emotion's primitive dictation is actually the heart of true autonomy.

CHAPTER III

EVERYONE HAS PROBLEMS

One day as I turned the pages of a magazine I came upon a tongue-in-cheek definition of what a specialist is. It said he is ". . . a person who knows very much about very little, and continues to learn more and more about less and less, until eventually he knows practically everything about almost nothing at all."

This may have too much malice and too little logic in it to be convincing, but it does hint at the problem the expert presents to the person involved in average activities, which do not include the splitting of hairs to arrive at obscure conclusions. It does suggest, however, that it might be useful to remap neurosis for the busy layman; to outline a picture that shows its central meaning, not its elaborate fringes of detailed involvements, but the root and rationale of its hold upon humanity.

Try It Simple First and Specialize Only Later
Many of us are not in a position to deal with the type of equations that stand for what we are pleased to call the miracles of science. As such we do not find them easily intelligible to us. We want to attain knowledge

we can translate into action that will make life livable. What we most need is to get at the essence of neurosis and its eradication as simply and directly as possible. So we ask ourselves, can we "learn the art of living" easily and clearly enough to parallel an architect's design, a business company's manifest, recipes for a good dinner, or the elements of contract bridge?

After all, the main point is that though our own emotions bully us, it is still wonderful to have emotions. They certainly give us our best experiences, and also most of the worst. The answer is to prime ourselves with enough useful knowledge of what emotions are and how they work so that we can constantly raise the averages on a satisfying and rewarding use of them. It is not too difficult to learn what has gone wrong and why it has done so; although setting it right doesn't just happen. It must be done, just as one has to learn golf or tennis, and to read and write.

There seems to be a resistance to the simple. Is it because simplicity doesn't flatter the ego enough? Undoubtedly, if we will admit that the ego is the reaction pattern of the defense we build over the effect upon us of the negative conditioning we have been subjected to.

A small group of us were discussing matters and things one evening, when someone suggested the idea that we declare what we thought ourselves to be, good-tempered or good-natured. The results were interesting. One man felt that he was good-tempered, but not good-natured. Another would admit to neither quality. Still another got into an uncertainty that became rather comic, wishing to claim both characteristics, and floundering in an effort to get away from an unflattering confession.

The experiment showed up rather neatly the human dilemma about the vagueness of our self-knowledge, and the consistent interference of the ego in an effort to attempt a calm estimate of our degree of emotional

31

evolution or devolution. The first man may have been near the truth, if we can consider being good-tempered as the sounder quality of the two, since being good-natured seems to imply a response manifesting a lack of keenness, as in the implication of the term "good-natured slob." The second man hid himself in the noncommittal. The third displayed utter confusion and staggered verbally to protect his self-esteem.

Having been born into a family intent upon seeking out the meaning of emotional disturbance and looking for the principles of its alleviation, one factor seemed to me to stand out prominently: the divergence between the research attitude of the exhaustive study of neurosis, and the quite different goal of viewing it as something for the individual to learn how to recognize and to get rid of.

Two Factors To Keep Separate

There are two factors that should be kept separate in our minds in regard to this new and long-needed approach to personal education relative to the problem of emotion and its command over life. First, the collecting of detailed information of the analyst must be valued for its own essential contribution; and second, the aim of the therapist, the "repair man," must be seen as more creative than statistical. The counselee's need rests more on synthesis than analysis. Thomas Troward put the importance of distinguishing between the use of analytic and creative processes in one succinct sentence: "Analysis that does not lead to synthesis is merely destructive."

In other words, analysis of a neurosis takes a person apart, but his most pressing need is to be "put together." The neurosis, with its tendency either to scatter one's attention or focus it too intently on unhappy experience, and the constant demand it puts upon the person for knowledge he just doesn't have, pulls him to pieces by the frustration and confusion it produces. To try to cure a scattered condition with a scattering method can easily turn into a mere delaying process, a waste of time. This it has often done.

A therapist's most useful relation to the individual, and the individual's to him, would seem to be a far cry from the splitting of hairs, learning lists of mental mechanisms and the remote interpretations of human vagaries. The counselor, who, granted, must know his subject if he is to fire the counselee with the desire needed to free himself from the load of confused concepts under which he labors, must also by some means summon the powerful attitude of enthusiasm so necessary to accomplish that purpose. Enthusiasm implies increased interest. That alone will lure him into the effort that can stir up the belief that he can be free of the fetters of emotional enslavement. For the nature and intensity of a person's beliefs determine the outcome of his life experience.

In the work of the therapist, the element of personal communication and explanation, the subtle handling of the reaction and mood of the counselee, the sensitive responsibility of the transference (confidence in the counselor) override in importance the assembling of facts and uninspiring review of mathematical evaluations. The latter can be of use in the research atmosphere, but not equally so in the counseling chamber.

We Are All in This Together

Under the exactitudes of specialization, the concept of neurosis became almost overnight a word bandied about from pillar to post, sucking up added variation from every mind it touched and finally its simple meaning was more or less lost in an avalanche of long words and elaborate mystifications. But in the end the central fact about this symptom of emotional confusion is that every child born into the human race is subject to its delimiting influence. It does not single out one person here and another there to attack. It moves in on every one of us, through the influences that play upon us from the cradle to the grave. It can be fairly said that no person can escape it utterly, for it has a basic relation to our common lack of effective knowledge about the forces of feeling and the tricks of thought.

But this truth of our universal exposure to the contagion of neurosis can bring us a sense of relief. We know that we are creatures who must learn, and we do not think of ignorance as hopeless but with confidence that it can be dealt with. There are even some of us who have already escaped many of the rigors of neurosis, because the early conditioning has been positive to a more than usual degree.

In using the word conditioning we have taken a step toward bringing the contour of neurosis into clear perspective. In other words, putting aside for the moment the undoubted truth that the full explanation of neurosis requires an array of complexity piled upon complexity, the really important thing is to know what its main root is, and leave the trunk, branches, and twigs to be understood by degrees, if the individual so desires and decrees. But we should all understand what the root of poorly managed thought and emotion is, for "first-things-first" is, or should be, the universally accepted rule in any branch of learning. You don't start a young student, not even an Einstein, with higher mathematics before you present him with the multiplication table.

So the conditioning — that is, the quantity of negative or undigestible impressions made on the individual by the particular experience of his early years — is the arrow pointing to the meaning of neurosis. If one has been trained (conditioned) on a basis of methods prompted by wisdom and love in reasonable balance, he can escape the worst dangers of maladjustment. In essence, then, neurosis is the natural result of unwise or misleading treatment and instruction imposed upon the dependent child. Thus utter freedom from neurosis is ridiculous to ask for.

Everyone is subjected to unfortunate conditioning, and there is no such thing as a perfect parent. We can, however, expect to grow out of the limiting ideas, habits, and beliefs that make up the most serious drawbacks of neurotic confusion. We can, if we will, return more and more to intelligent living, free of the many "mechanisms," the exaggerations of thinking and feeling, that have been named and defined as neurotic rather than normal.

But to gain this release we must set up some means by which we can gain sound but simple understanding of thought and emotion, either in school or out of it. As a matter of fact, we must search for it. Since better command of these two great human powers is a daily developing need in human experience not covered in the schools, we must still see it as an essential part in the field of learning.

Neurosis is ill-conceived and poorly handled human reaction. It can become a veritable nemesis, but its possible point of no return can be understood and avoided.

Keys to What Emotionalism Feels Like

The key to what neurosis "feels like" could be diluted down to degrees of rage at life, fear of life, hatred of life, or disastrous misinterpretation of life. And in this connection, we must feel free to treat life and people as synonyms, for to a human being, unless he departs for an uninhabited island, people and their conditioning are a very high proportion of his experience in living.

In other words, neurosis is the inner struggle in every human being between his sense-of-identity (his true nature) and the necessary command over his all-powerful basic emotions: rage, fear, sex and wonder.

All four of them crave expression, and start at a very early age to try out any and every means of gaining their fulfillment. Instinct and energy force him to act, but ignorance makes him make mistakes. Much too often he is given no helpful explanation of why they *are* mistakes, so the confusion between his impulse to act, to try, to discover, and the constant balking of that impulse, arouse a natural resistance expressed by the negative aspects of his emotional power.

So restraint and punishment are inevitable, and confusion — the main trigger of neurotic reaction — too often starts the habit of blind inner rebellion. This often then tends to turn into emotional habits based more on that resistance than on a sensible understanding of the logical demands of livable human relationships. The identity sense is thus diverted from workable appraisals of what is required to build a satisfactory life. Having no very lucid picture of sane living, and irritated by an example full of contradictions from his elders, the child attempts to set up a "one-man" process of his own. Naturally it won't work. To enjoy life we must get along with other people.

The power of the identity-drive inherent in all of us has often frightened philosophers into declaring it dangerous. And so it is if it is forced to stand at bay and fight for what it loves and needs. Preachers have demanded that we sacrifice it. Parents have punished it. The law tries to quell it by restraint. But willy-nilly — for it has the strength and majesty of the Creator behind it — we secretly if not openly go on seeking one thing: ourselves; dreaming of releasing one thing: ourselves; needing to protect one thing: ourselves. And when a thousand centuries have passed, this story will still be new. We shall go on seeking that one thing: ourselves.

A Most Vital Fact To Remember

However, at this point it is vitally important to remember

that this does not necessarily deter us from consideration for others. In fact, it is perfectly obvious that we crave affection, and that our desire impulses are locked in a deep urge to care for other people and receive affection from them. How fortunate for us that this saving grace of balance already exists within the human organism, made up of the strong urge toward one's own growth and success in life, and the yearning for love and respect from others. Unfortunately, in the young this compelling need for love and understanding has been exploited or rebuffed in countless cases to ease the lives of parents and free them to live by the dictum, "Do as I say, not as I do."

The anxiety about unbridled self-love developing in the child has come mostly from the misuse of fear, which prompted moralists to accent insistently the bogey of selfishness, and ignore the human impulse to please. The frustration which resulted encouraged rather than discouraged true selfishness, for since the instinct of self-preservation is provided for the purpose of pro-tecting the individual, it will attempt to do just that. Its automatic force must use any agent it finds handy, and the untutored child cannot be expected to manifest the wisdom and restraint of a St. Francis. Neither, as I understand it, did St. Francis until he had lived and learned.

Of course the pressure from that very life-saving instinct of self-preservation has often interfered with the development of generosity, which, though it is a natural expression of the emotion of love, needs assurance of fair play if it is to avoid the hot pursuit of self-interest. And that assurance should be protected to a reasonable degree by parents, with wise counsel and explicit assurance that they are for the child, even though they may ques-tion some of his actions and punish him if he persists in them.

The natural, benevolent impulses must be effectively understood and sustained, but, being prompted by love rather than rage is an automatically active tool of the self-preserving instinct. Otherwise they may become enervated before the child is old enough to comprehend their irreplaceable value, to himself and to the development of life.

We need to see first of all that self-development is an obligation to life, not a sin, and that every evil impulse (except in the abnormal emotional imbalance of degenerates or psychotics) has a virtue to balance it. That virtue will tend to develop naturally unless either too much injustice or too lulling a favoritism fixates the child's attention on his rights and no one else's.

There is a truth about neurosis, a method of clarifying the problems it presents; and it couldn't be simpler. It is to make a practice of asking oneself the question "Why?" in relation to any difficulty, disappointment, or deprivation connected with other people. This question, "Why?" is the main entrance into the subjective area of living, a realm needing much more of our effort if we are to get straight about life and make it more worthwhile. And if we stubbornly refuse to face our possible part in contributing to a human tangle of whatever sort, when it is being aggravated by our own neurotic concepts or actions, strife could go on forever. At least we should admit to ourselves that we might be acting neurotically. If we then firmly assert, "I am not my neurosis," it can clear the air so that one can begin to root out twisted emotional beliefs and attitudes.

Answers to the question "Why?" lead to the very center of Life: that is, to cause; or could we say "the because of" our experiences. For cause is Life's central process, what it uses to bring everyone and everything into existence. Understanding cause can answer our whys, but only if we are willing to watch its action in our lives and admit the inevitable consequences it produces. (*"Why* did this happen? Did I have a part in setting it off?")

We should start to think of ourselves as separate from our neurotic ways of reacting, for remembering that a person is not his neurosis, we can give up any sense of being singled out as somehow peculiar. For the neurosis is not one's actual self, but a distortion of reactions due to the misunderstandings so typical of it. This changes the picture very radically, for embarrassment over admitting being neurotic can be utterly cast aside.

It will take courage at first to give true answers to a good many whys, for we identify with neurotic habits as though they represented our own natures identically. But the fact is that the more one comes to understand the truths about this problem, the less painful it becomes to face the necessary admissions: the time-wasting, and, yes, often idiotic habits or attitudes we have built up to "save face" or protect our identities in the give-and-take of life.

Rediscovering One's Identity

When we realize that we personally are not basically responsible for our habits of evasion, rationalization, hidden self-depreciation, or outlandish self-glorification, the whole process of rediscovering our personal identity becomes entertaining as well as gradually producing many increased satisfactions. The main thing we are responsible for is leaving ourselves captive in the bog of misconceptions that have made us uneasy, resentful, and lacking in normal self-knowledge. Release demands a pretty sharp review of our basic attitudes, to see if they are truly ours or carelessly assumed to enjoy the ease of sliding down the line of least resistance.

We talk a lot about willpower, but do not succeed in making use of it because we do not stop and think when we are told that "the will obeys the image in the mind." An image, not of "I will" but of "I want" must come from the motive center of the mind before the will can act. The will doesn't know what to do until we tell it, by forming an image of what we want and holding it in our minds.

To stabilize the human identity there needs to be a knowledge of, respect for, and constant awareness of cause and its creative effect upon human consciousness. We should all have been schooled to understand that training ourselves to live by cause first and effect second could ultimately clear out of life nine-tenths of the habit of confusion and wasted time that now afflicts us so dismally.

If a husband does not have knowledge of how to recognize the cause of any troublesome quarrel with his wife, he is badly equipped to be a husband. The same is true of wives in their own relation to life and to their mates. A quarrel can start, proceed for weeks, end in divorce, and the lonely confusion of both partners because they did not, or would not, seek the cause of the difficulty, admit it, and generously forget it; or else examine it, get to understand it, and honestly search for a mutual adjustment.

The ego has too often prevented any chance of a simple sane handling of a problem that may be annoying, which can easily be the silliest possible thing on which to allow a marriage to crash.

The ego can be a very sore spot at the center of consciousness, from hurt feelings, rage at injustices, fear of abandonment by others, or just boredom from not knowing how to discover and use one's complete identity. But before the search for the self is freed from the danger of either self-adoration or self-abasement, a person must move to the point of choosing some exterior value to which he will relate that self, some cause or meaning outside the self, or it has no way to "prove up" on its own value.

The self cannot prove its value just by asserting it; it must be gauged by something other than itself, to which it gives allegiance, and demonstrates that allegiance by discernment and loyalty. Without that balancing factor of belief in *something* greater than the human being, manifesting love and wisdom behind the present scope of mankind, and knowing answers to our dilemmas which we can discover only by growth in understanding and practice in positive living, we are without a dependable gauge for self-expression.

This need for comprehending that there is *something* greater than ourselves is why it is so essential that we become as aware of Cause as the Source of our life as we are aware of hunger; that we learn to understand the vital part of relating ourselves to Cause. We are important to Life, as well as worthy of the enjoyment of our own value. It is possible, though perhaps difficult with our inadequately conceived education, to enjoy success without becoming a fool entranced with his own folly. But intelligent appreciation of success is essential to the job of succeeding. If there is no anticipation of enjoyment behind effort, it will not continue to be vital for very long.

Progress in moving forward toward the higher octaves of our four basic emotions — a constructive use of energy (from rage), dependable judgment (from fear), compassionate attitudes (from love), and an adequate intelligence (from wonder) — will protect us from the gnawing misery of self-dissatisfaction. It is the only way the natural interest in the self can be guaranteed against a dry rot of soul (not to speak of the clinical threat), which takes on preoccupation with a self that relates to nothing and no one but itself.

What does it mean to say, "God is not mocked"? It

is a poetic way of stating that Cause cannot be disregarded or abused with impunity. Cause is Life, in the basic sense. It is boss. It must be understood and obeyed, or its greatest effect known to us — humanity — is in constant danger. Cause reacts with nonacceptance upon all that mocks it, as the immutable law that "action and reaction are equal" indicates.

The intent in any action produces a consistent consequence. An unkind remark is made to someone to whom one has an intimate relation and love cannot respond although rage may be suppressed if any love exists. Too many times the capacity for love is not strong enough to weather the experience without returning rage for rage. We "mock" Cause in our belittling and degrading of the word and the condition of love; yet showing our insatiable interest in love's power by our very reiteration of the word. This is indeed a precarious "mocking of God." It is useful to ask ourselves the simple question of what we believe life would be like if both wisdom and love were whisked away never to return. Simplicity has an effect on us that sophistication can try in vain to break. As Cause it remains forever constant.

Troward's concept, "Analysis that does not lead to synthesis is merely destructive," is another way of saying we must return to Cause, mentally and emotionally, often enough to keep our relation to life stable. For effects represent mere multiplicity and threaten confusion; whereas Cause provides that out of which effects can be produced. It is stable in nature and creative in purpose. It is the very core of life.

If we are right in seeing nurture as a meaningful symbol more consistent with the essence of woman, and wisdom as the truest and most basic potentiality of man, then we must expect neglect of either causal quality to bring destructive, not constructive, results. A man cannot defy the nature of his basic meaning — his causal quality of potential wisdom — and receive true benefit from it. A woman cannot refuse to offer nurture to life and its individuals, and be of any great value as a woman. There may be other things she can be, but not a representative of woman's most far-reaching quality: the warm recuperative assurance that only love can give.

Understanding of the identity-drive is basic psychology in the study of youth or age. Until we accept this truth and become ready to build life in relation to it, we shall continue to fail in any attempt to establish a sound environment for a human society. Any government not based on an intelligent acceptance of the creative sovereignty of the human identity-drive will inevitably run up against its adverse power, and fail to succeed as a permanent community.

Historically, this has been proved over and over again. But the individual will have to accept his share in making this work. There could hardly be a simpler piece of logic than to say that it will never work — it cannot — unless somehow each individual can become deeply enough acceptant of the fact that success requires that he constantly reach for a developed expression of his basic emotions. For at their primitive level they are incapable of expression consistent with universal safety to life on Earth.

This understanding of the need to ally ourselves with constructive causes is the core of the dilemma of neurosis and its mechanisms, its meanings, and its natural existence. It is not a fatal disease, a disgrace, or a hopeless entrapment. It is a to-be-expected consequence of ignorance of the law of growth and the development of human understanding. Growth proceeds from underdevelopment, through the constructive use of personal ability, to improvement in individual and racial intelligence, health, and enjoyment of life.

It Is Fatal To "Fight Life"

To realize this process of improvement, we need to take a stand individually and collectively, to stop fighting life, which is to say stop encouraging negative causes. The greatest causes in the realm of meaning, the subjective aspect of life, are wisdom and love, as essentially indicated by man and woman in their balancing spheres of existence. We need to see that the universal law — action and reaction are equal — requires that to the best of our ability we give something of true value to these two great principles before we expect to fulfill our own desires.

A constant search for release from ignorance may be said to be the basic answer to ridding life of neurosis, which, it seems more and more obvious, contributes damagingly to producing many of our physical ills. It certainly produces nervous tension, and tension is generally accepted as detrimental to the health of the body.

Neurosis, then, is not a new malady that has suddenly appeared out of nowhere. Our attention to it has suddenly burst into life. It has been with us always, but appears more than usually strange to us because it affects those two invisibilities — thought and feeling. We are coming more and more to the conclusion that the central enemy we must all deal with is ignorance. If we were not so unaware of the tremendous importance of knowing how to understand our own thought and emotion, their misuse could be gradually eliminated. It is a job to be done; and in fact, to many of those who have applied themselves to gathering and using such knowledge, it is a fascinating game.

Do most of us ever really spend any appreciable time in sensibly examining how and why we express rage, how often we give in to fear unnecessarily, how much we desire to nurture life wherever it touches us? And, most of all, do we admit that we cannot expect to be free of trouble unless we constantly seek for effective methods that fit the needs of increasing sound wisdom and genuine love?

Constructive humility, not self-abasement, is a productive and very much needed mental habit to stabilize humanity. Correctly used it is the balance wheel to shape the effervescent creative force of still immature but always dynamic mankind.

When a person wakes up to the fact that he must accept as a pristine duty the job of learning what "first things first" means, he will attain a habit of mental balance. And if, while he provides himself with protective armor against danger to his life, he gives equal time to the kind of procedure that will bring about the reliable handling of his own emotions, he will have the answers to all of his humanly solvable dilemmas — yes, all!

CHAPTER IV

DISTORTED EMOTIONS

A Wise Man's Realization

Charles Darwin, with his power of thought honed to a sharp edge by concentrated study, stated that "the highest possible stage of moral culture is when we recognize that we ought to control our thought." We psychologists would like to see the verb "direct" substituted for "control," for we want to see the extraordinary talents of men and women released and wisely directed. But let's not look at such a fine bit of understanding critically. Let's welcome it gratefully as an important concept about how to increase our better handling of experience.

We have accomplished much and we can do greater things, if we sense the importance of Darwin's conclusion in this special instance. But to get the full meaning of his inspired idea, let us say that it is poorly handled emotion, inadequately understood and inspired by thought, that brings most of the human aspect of trouble into life.

In the United States not a day passes in which humane actions do not occur: the giving of money to the needy, neighborly sharing of duties and acts of generosity, the offering of comfort in misfortune. But when someone's personal attitudes or beliefs are scorned or opposed, a wild passion to defend them is usually roused. Arguments are begun that have no chance whatever of proving anything of merit, for under such circumstances everything is heard, if indeed heard at all, through the automatic resistance of the force of the misuse of rage trying to quell the fear of having been wrong in one's own convictions.

It does not occur to people in the thrall of fear's handy weapon, which is rage, that if a fact or principle exists, no torrent of words can destroy its authenticity. It exists or it does not, and words about it are only useful to clarify its meaning and contribution more fully. Only listening alertly and commenting reasonably will train one to respond to a truth, or a portion of one, with the calm scrutiny essential to clear thinking. Such listening can save a person endless time and a lot of high blood pressure. A babble of heated defense will only push the blood pressure higher.

To learn, one must listen. The mind is also listening when we are reading; that is, if we train it to. We are losers if we try to cover up ignorance. All we are left with is a meager supply of knowledge; and knowlege is the food the mind depends on for vitality and safety. Touchy fear of not being right is a favorite neurotic reaction, for insecurity as to one's own worth is powerfully represented in almost any neurotic constellation.

An animal will fight and die for food, sex, and security as assurances of his continued existence. Man differs from the animal in one great essential. Added to this trio of urges, he owns a fourth basic drive: he will fight fiercely for his power of choice. He claims the right to a separate and independent decision as to what sort of food, sex, and security are to be his. He desires to choose by what means he shall expand his life and assure his identity. We are human because of that will to choose.

So, most of us having lived through severe friction in attaining permission to exercise a portion of our power of choice, we need something as specific as a technique to free ourselves from the habits of early conditioning that have limited our wise use of free choice.

If we have the interest, the courage, and the recognition of the value to us of starting to understand our emotions more fully, we can change any attitudes we have taken on that stem from neurosis. Only the development of thought and emotion, reasonably free of the deformation of ideas the negatively conditioned ego deals in, will be capable of forming imagery that can understand what the needs of a worthwhile life are.

A First Step to Escape Emotional Enslavement

Clearing our minds of superimposed neurotic attitudes is in fact a first and primary method of release from the handicap of being emotionally enslaved, and thereby threatened with illness of body or mind. So it would be wise to start thinking about basic emotion, so that its traits and trends become familiar to us. It would ultimately show us how much can be gained in preventing exaggerated feeling from so often putting us in jeopardy.

A central factor in the action of the realm of feeling is to form itself into attitudes, which then, right or wrong, it will defend almost to the death. Attitudes can be like an anchor to a ship. They can stop all progress forward, if they are crystallized on wrong belief. They then have a tendency to halt our development as individuals and as a society. As a matter of fact, a mental technique is mainly a storm trooper to break up the initial opposition to effective thought imposed by negative mental habits, such as self-disparagement (inferiority complex), feeling threatened (persecution complex), a desperate sense of one's desires always being denied (frustration complex), habits of giving irrational excuses and "crying before one is hurt" (rationalization and defense mechanism).

When set out in a row, these mental trends may sound rather trumped up, but they are common mental-emotional twists, and they are all neurotic; that is, based on a poor handling of personal feeling from little or no worthwhile understanding of rage, fear, sex, and wonder. We really don't know what to do with them to keep their tremendous powers and skills from pulling and pushing us in fruitless directions.

The first and greatest technique to get rid of neurosis, then, would be to straighten out our attitudes. For if they include a considerable number which oppose a truly sensible and effectual understanding of life, our thus-hampered process of image-making will unfailingly lead us into harmful, not healthful habits. That unbreakable link between the image and the will, which takes over the job of fulfilling the image and quite naturally reflecting the person's attitudes, can only tend to perpetuate any false convictions that are lodged emotionally in his mind. It will prevent him from freeing himself from nervous-emotional errors of judgment and types of impulse so typical of neurosis, unless he understands the power of the image and sets his mind to refusing any disadvantageous command it puts upon him.

People in general fairly beg for help with their difficulties, but they balk when suggestions for ridding themselves of neurotic complaints are offered. And we can hardly deny that there is a somewhat exasperating nuisance factor in being told one must start on a course of therapy as an adult when one already has his hands, mind, and body occupied with the job of living.

This reluctance to roll up our mental and emotional sleeves and take on the job of getting rid of neurosis is understandable, for we have been exhausting ourselves since childhood with the consequences of misguided thinking and negatively aroused emotions. We are caught in the paradox of the results of our errors getting in the way of our chance to correct them. We ourselves have set the trip wire for our own tumbles, but we feel abused when asked to pick ourselves up.

However, when we once get an idea of how much relief we can experience from changing neurotic habits to constructive workable ones, the matter takes on a different aspect. A foolish, injurious, unfair, anxious or untrue belief can be given up while washing dishes, playing golf, traveling to work, trimming the hedge, and so on and on. All it takes is opening the mind to the value of looking, just really looking, at some pet habit, like wasting the energy of rage on trifles and false premises. A calm and quiet reestimation of attitude, in regard to believing in allowing oneself to have fling after fling of unbridled emotion, will reveal it as contrary to common sense. Unguided fury, terror, lust, and inquisitiveness act like germs; they bring on illness sooner or later.

"Bad" Is Not Fatal, and "Good" Is Not Limited

If we wish to ease our lives by getting more pleasure and less pain out of the endowments of emotion, we should always have a certain thought in the back of our minds. And that thought is that human nature is set up on a basis of duality: good or bad, constructive or destructive, pleasing or displeasing, maturing or undeveloped. This is especially true of emotion. However, we use these terms only in a relative sense. The qualities of human nature are not actually static; they are developmental, made so by the power of choice. A designation of good or bad is relative, for whether one uses the power of choice for personal evolution or devolution, the book is never closed on the nature of the outcome. The direction an emotion takes can always be changed. So bad is not fatal, and good is not limited.

RAGE

Basic rage is a source of energy provided for protection of the race and the individual within it. There is a developed counterpart of rage, which we call courage, an impulse fortified by thought, to act with a positive value added. Rage and courage are intrinsically the same impulse. To the challenge of a disturbing situation an individual is as capable of courage as of rage, in proportion to the development of his capacity to choose. In other words, the energy of rage can be expressed as courage, if the mind of the individual provides his will with a mental image to show what the desired action is. It all depends upon the trend of the person's power of choice.

This is an area where one's health or tendency toward illness is greatly affected, and can be assisted by methods or techniques.

For example:

If you feel your blood beginning to boil, to keep command of your emotions, no matter how incongruous and inappropriate it may seem, smile or laugh good-naturedly. Force yourself to. It can be done with practice. Whatever the point of discussion is, consider the protection of your future health and take it easy. You can't laugh good-naturedly without relaxing the tension you have gotten into. We know too little about when to give a little in order to gain a lot, but it is a valuable habit to cultivate.

It is foolish to force your blood pressure up from the fear of showing ignorance, or even defending a worthwhile conviction. You will only lose the argument anyway, or it will end in stalemate if your rage arouses that of your opponent. Don't waste your energy in anger by defying the laws of emotional reaction. You can use it for something more worth your while. A raised voice is a perfect invitation to an opponent to either walk away or precipitate a brawl. Of course, if you want a brawl, good luck, and may the best man win.

FEAR

The emotion of fear is inclined to be a "hanger-back." It will hide behind rage if rage accepts being summoned to help it. Or, if the individual has gained some control over negative emotional reaction, reason can get a word in and present positive images to his mind that will show him a better way to handle the situation in which fear is floundering.

It is easy to burst into violent defense of your ideas or concepts but it is hard to avoid the aftermath. Primitive fury once started is pretty difficult to stop. Rage provides energy, but tends to get the bit in its teeth. Take your hidden fear, that is manifesting through rage, out on physical prowess of some sort. The satisfaction of enjoyable action can drain the fear and start one back to a sensible mood. The point is to replace the fury with activity that has a positive purpose. During this process, invite reason in to arbitrate. Don't just sit and simmer, assuring yourself of how wronged you have been.

Ask yourself why you feel you must be as furious about a certain thing as you are. Changing your mind is not a mental felony. If you are not afraid to change it, you may find there is no need to. It is one's neurosis that is so pitifully fearful. It is lack of confidence in oneself that is so frightening that it rouses fury, and spoils the possibility of viewing the situation sanely. The analyses of some of the psychoses, so-called, come close to describing unbridled rage, when actually they are based on a torturing fear.

Take as suspect too great a quantity of emotion in a given reaction. A great deal of the time exaggerated feeling is caused by an emotional flare-up from some incident in the past. This is why we make such a point of the past in the present. It is a primary key to the burden of neurosis. To have subconscious memory play the trick on you of adding the pain of past experiences to present dilemmas has a serious effect on a present experience. You can reduce it, however, by tracing past painful experiences and turning them one by one out of your mind.

To allow fright or self-pity from something long past and over with to crowd into the present scene and intensify it is just dumb. Let it go, consciously and insistently. Refuse to allow past injustices or cruelties to keep cropping up and animating present situations. They are extremely bad for your health, and you are wasting life by remaining in their power.

For example:

Refuse to let fear keep summoning rage to go on wild goose chases. And keep your voice down. If it is too loud, it will incite the emotions of your vis-a-vis to a goose chase of his or her own rage, which becomes the perpetrator of the famous all-day or all-night arguments. Nobody involved ever actually listens to what is said in a shrill or strident voice, their blood pressure merely goes up. They feel threatened and their reason dies on the vine.

LOVE

The emotion of love is a sensitive and vulnerable one because it is embedded in a whole gamut of human reactions that go deep into the well-being and happiness of the human race. Its vital relation to sexuality, however, is so potent a power that love itself, the subjective goal of this wonderful emotion, is hampered in its development by the immediacy of the sexual function and its satisfactions. But it is obvious that while the act may bring momentary fulfillment, the life is often cheated of very real and desirable joys. And for women especially, who symbolize this emotion, intensely longed-for possibilities are left wanting in a man's world, where impersonal emotions and attitudes are the more typical and it is mostly the physical function of love that is given full attention.

Our haphazard use of language, our lack of real attention to what the more important words mean, adds constantly to the confusion human life gets into. How many of us stop to think about generosity and what it means? Do we realize that no one actually loves unless he or she, in meeting problems of disagreement, is always ready to offer what can honestly be offered to another? That is generosity, and utterly consistent with love. Such an attitude can so ameliorate the pressures of disagreement that it can be lessened many degrees and more usefully resolved. We are a long way from living up to the claims we make by declaring we love when we don't even know what the elements of love are.

But whatever the lacks in humanity's development, the main need lies very centrally in getting rid of the strange habits that neurosis builds. Such habits produce their disturbing ways in relation to almost any human situation one may be involved in. Inferiority weighs heavily on the success of love and marriage by its doubts and fears. It also aims a severe blow at business competence. Frustration plants a hedge of nervous preoccupation that tarnishes the bright hopes of sex and love. Persecution feeling can almost cut off the chances of interesting, enthusiastic, affectionate communication between two married people. Rationalization and defense mechanism can often make a marriage partner seem a strange unsatisfactory person to his mate, when after all it's only the neurosis.

The interference with one's chances of making a mate relation that can rise above life's wear and tear come, as with most other problems, from the mishandling of emotion. And the larger proportion of failure can be blamed on the neurotic distortions in the areas of rage and fear; for these two useful but tricky powers are more natively threatening than nurture (love) and origination (wonder). In fact, it is rage and fear that are aroused when love and curiosity are challenged. They are the restraining or protective agents when any factor of the personality is in trouble or just uneasy.

But the greatest danger of any exaggeration of the normal responses of these two emotions comes in most cases from twisted attitudes, from overreacting in one's relation to others because of neurotic attitudes picked up in the growing-up period that were not reasonably explained at the time. They might right themselves automatically in the adult years if the subconscious did not have what we might call so "closed" a memory, and the nervous system such sensitive reactions. The subconscious does not always give up the most painful memories, nor the nervous system the sharpest sensations of fright or injustice. They must be dug up, more intelligently understood, and induced to change.

For example:

In any serious enough threat to the mate relation,

the husband and wife should reach for positive responses from their basic symbols: he for discernment or wisdom, she for love or nurture. The impulses of love are woman's great gift to life. If she reverses love into hate, no adjustment can be found until she returns to the nourishment of love.

In any foreboding altercation with his wife the wisest thing the husband can do, whatever else he may do, would be to interpose judiciously at proper intervals an assertion of some sort indicating his love for her. It is very likely that he will be unable to get her attention in any other way. Even if at the moment he is pretty sure he doesn't love her, if he did once love her it is a commendable, benign gamble to resurrect it. If it won't rise to that bait, reconciliation is unlikely anyway, but it can't be done with one "I love you" only. What we glibly refer to as the humanity in people demands bonafide assurances by means of repetition. One thing is certain, if it really is a serious difference reconciliation never will be attained if none of the positive sides of emotion are offered: generosity, patience, and admission of genuine misdemeanors.

And the wife, if she expects to get her husband's attention in an effective way, had better praise him for being fair. It could entice him into being so, for it is one of wisdom's main goals. The key is, don't expect a mate to respond to hate with love. It is a very difficult thing to do, and entirely uncertain to depend upon.

WONDER

Wonder, or curiosity, is the great center of possible emancipation for mankind. Being milder and less specifically emotional than any of the other three sensibility responses, it can escape to some degree the prod of passion that makes most emotion top-heavy. Nevertheless, it can respond with inexhaustible enthusiasm according to what type of interest fires the imagination, stirs the love, or involves the defense impulses of fear and rage in an individual.

For example:

Less friction tends to come from the misuse of the emotion of wonder than from any other. But if it does, it is apt to be a destructive division in the attention people pay to each other — in marriage, family relationships, friendships, and between sweethearts. If the typical goals of curiosity differ in individuals, they may well lead two people in differing directions and thus come up against emotional, mental, or geographical separations that preclude physical companionship. If the interest factor fits a certain person's nature, it is pretty sure to cause a very real problem in his congeniality. It is difficult to maintain interest in someone who shows no interest in oneself, or has too difficult a time doing it. If the curiosity impulses differ too widely in a married couple, the strain can be hard on both. If one or both are rugged, well-balanced and unusually understanding, an adjustment may be possible. But if marriage is involved, the risk should be honestly faced before the impossible is asked of either person.

We cannot expect anything as tremendous as love to come when we whistle. It offers too much to be treated cavalierly.

This quartet of emotional impulses and responses is the essence of sentience in the living being, what we might call its true "livingness." It is impossible to think of human creatures being worth much without the four great dynamic influences: rage, fear, sex, and wonder, and their developmental powers. They provide the immense drama of life, and it is our obligation to take and guide them by that elusive, all but indefinable but most potent emanation: the Spirit in man.

That mysterious intangibility, Spirit, though seemingly formless and beyond our physical scope, is still the element with the final power to decide the fate of mankind. The emotions partake of Its invisibility and Its reign over those things in life that are most meaningful though unseen. They are in some observable, if obscure, sense the body of life's intense reality.

CHAPTER V

ELIMINATING FALSE GUILT

Guilt Manifests in Two Forms

The discovery in recent years of significant aspects of neurosis has required us to take a new view of the question of personal guilt. For it appears that there are two conditions of guilt rather than one. There is genuine guilt, which may be defined as acts against life and its progress. Then there is false guilt: a fiction of the mind, brought about by adults inadvertently misrepresenting to growing children what their conduct means in relation to virtue.

The common phrases used to scold a child sound so ordinary, so harmless. But the repeated accusation in them can build an oppressive sense of always being wrong. There is a tone of voice used in this time-honored custom that plants fear in the subconscious mind. The words themselves may not mean much. It is the tone of voice that contains the power of threat. It sounds too convincingly like trouble to come.

A sense of guilt might almost be claimed to be the root reaction of what we call neurosis. In the search for the causes of emotional troubles in men and women carried on by Freud and his followers, masses of guilty feeling appeared in the histories of the people examined.

And it was quite obvious that this hidden sense of guilt was primarily based on early experiences that made a deep enough impression on the child's mind to remain in his subconscious as a threat. One of the most pathetic varieties is exemplified by the pollution complex, in which the child, from impressions induced by the "hell-fire" preaching of past years, was terrified by dire predictions. In one case, an adult woman, thoroughly exhausted from caring for her fast failing father, fell asleep and found him dead when she wakened. Her intense feeling of guilt took the form of a compulsion to wash everything before she used it, her distraught mind entertaining an absurd image of wrongdoing, and then embodying itself in an absurdity.

The impartial analyst, working with the individual and being given all the facts that are supposed to prove the guilt, can seldom see adequate justification for its being considered guilt in the true sense. To him these supposed guilty deeds have little or no relation to an act against life. They are almost always in fact an act against his convenience or the parent's ego. In this way the tragedy of a person's becoming imprisoned in false guilt can be discovered, and its harmful influence on the life of the person affected by it be revealed.

It is this mistaken feeling of being at fault that most needs to be explained and removed in treating a neurosis so that the resentment, the rage, the forlorn loneliness, the desperate effort to cover up the load of guilty fears in his memory, will begin to let go their stranglehold on a person's subconscious attention, and set him free to have more natural reactions. As a matter of fact, most of the strange fears people carry around with them through life are based on a twisted notion of being somehow guilty. It is rarely true guilt, which must be put to the proof and judged by reason and solid evidence if it is to be seen as actual wrongdoing.

Such profound suggestibility, typical of the emotional depths of human beings, shows how important to life is the emotional stability of a parent. It outweighs many of the social goals on which so much time, energy, and money are spent: prestige based on money, good looks rather than goodwill, ingenuity used to defraud, and the like.

Every person carrying a load of mistaken guilt from early life is threatened with unnecessary emotional discomforts later on. The less sensitive types resist the self-accusation that produces false guilt, and are more inclined toward misdemeanors representing true guilt. Those people luckily born to parents with well-balanced thought and feeling tend to succeed more easily in life: in business or profession, or in their personal lives — and perhaps in both. They do not have to struggle with a mistaken concept of personal guilt.

False guilt, then, is apt to be a central factor in emotional maladjustment, and it specifically implies impressionability: a quality typical of people capable of being civilized. Insensibility in a person does not induce a feeling of guilt. The born criminal is not bothered by it. His success in crime is generally a matter of pride to him. His feelings are calloused and do not trouble him when he steals, rapes, or kills. It is very possible that a good many criminals are in reality merely rebelling against a sense of false guilt.

It is probable that more of the criminal type are redeemable than we realize, but it is pretty certain that what we might call sensitive intelligence contributes largely to preventing downright criminality, while nevertheless being the breeding ground for a high percent of neurosis. Such a person tends to accuse himself rather than take out revenge for his discomfort on the world.

Cases of consequences of false guilt from a variety of causes are strongly indicated in biography, and especially autobiography. Hawthorne was a prey to morbid anxiety. A sentence written to his wife, as follows, indicates a pretty abnormal attitude of mind. "I do trust, my dearest, that you have been employing this bright day for both of us, for I have spent it in my dungeon and the only light that broke upon me was when I opened your letter." Mark Twain compensated for his anxiety through humor, but he lived all his life with fearful insecurity and a sense of guilt about himself. If anyone could have freed Nietzsche of his subjective phobia, we would have witnessed a mighty blossoming of genius. As it was, all he wrote is shadowed by abnormality.

False Guilt Is a Great Confuser

False guilt is a strange influence. It changes the average facts of reality and brings a kind of madness of unreality into ordinary experience. And always it is this frenzied emotion from the past that pulls the facts out of shape, and endows even a tone of voice with power enough to invoke the executioner. Because convulsive spasms of sudden reactions of false guilt are automatically hidden within an individual's thought and feeling, many unfair judgments are made about people. Those in the public view are inadvertently castigated by public censure for this misfortune of memory. Thus many who would not dream of striking a child are in truth "striking a child" by such action.

Cure can be brought to pass by the intensity of our realization of the part emotion can play in shackling us with imaginary guilt. Fear is magnified past all reason by the skill imagination has to surround the feeling of possible personal guilt with a series of images of retribution. And here it is important to remind ourselves that we are talking about guilt fears taken on in childhood.

We would not speak in such terms of adult guilt, whether true or false. That is an entirely different situation. The adult, faced with a plausible accusation, has his life training and experience to help him place his actual culpability in reasonable perspective. And yet even so, the sense of false guilt he may have developed in youth can enter into an adult situation, and, with its added unfounded fears, place an almost unendurable pressure on his nervous system.

Then too there is the disadvantage that his consternation, which may become evident to others, can affect their estimate of his status as a person, and he may be judged on the basis of his reaction to fears over which he has little control. This is because these invading anxieties have no logical relation to his present experience but appear "on their own," as it were, bringing with them their inexplicable feeling of being guilty.

Think of how exaggeratedly a child reacts to a minor disappointment. He cries as though his heart would break, while an adult would receive it with nothing more stormy than mild exasperation. This known truth measures the contrast between our buried memories of childhood's supposed sins and the adult's attitude regarding the same type of action. Unless we are able to recognize how furious our inner feelings are, we cannot free our subconscious processes from the imaginary delinquencies of the past.

There is of course much egotism in anxiety. In getting rid of fears based on imaginary guilt, everything depends on our not rushing to the defense of ourselves against the concept of false guilt. The first step is to see it as logical. The next is to keep to ourselves our efforts to free ourselves from it. Unhappily, we cannot very often risk taking anyone else into our confidence concerning the discovery of the evidences of fear and guilt. Even though we begin to understand that there is absolutely no sense in reanimating the self-accusations of past actions, it can devastate the possibility of cure if we admit ill-considered advice into these tender places in our minds.

The realization of what happens in a child's mental experiences that cramps his confidence in himself and life, even with all the discussion about it, is too new to have much effect on the thinking habits of society.

We are all egotists, no matter how agreeable we may seem. And when it comes to interrupting our own stream of consciousness to give really vital attention to the emotional sufferings of an associate, we are apt to drag out the old clichés: "Don't let it get you, guy"; "Better let that kind of thing alone, just brace up and forget it"; "Maybe the fellow who said, 'Let your mind alone,' knew what he was talking about . . ."

We cannot afford to subject ourselves to this kind of cavalier encouragement. There is no use exposing ourselves to such benign condescension. The factor of false guilt lurking in the subconscious mind is not a joke. It is a bitter reality in many a life, and its power to disturb a person's life, and sometimes destroy it, is a reality. It must be approached with serious intent and guarded from careless comment until there has been time and effort enough for the afflicted individual to exhibit at least his first smile at how he was helplessly gulled into a mistaken sense of false guilt.

But, in time, if we can discover a genuinely thinking soul, who has a real capacity for empathy, we should grab the opportunity to stretch our own understanding of how we can cut off the past-in-the-present reaction when it is negative. And then listen to any encouragement to recall and exorcise the memories of our youth that fostered a false belief in personal guilt. That way lies sanity and the ultimate cure of the exasperating nag of false-guilt uneasiness, which can interfere with the best laid plans of any one of us.

Memory Can Be Loaded with False Guilt

Memory is a priceless part of our mental endowment, but a good many of us can be justly said to have neurotic memories. Our reservoirs of recall contain too numerous a number of impressions of life that were unhappy, painful, or confusing to the point of creating false anxiety. This kind of mixed up learning process, building as it does our attitudes and beliefs about the meaning of life, puts demands for understanding on us that we can hardly be expected to have as small children. The result is mismanaged reactions and judgments in later years.

A most fortunate thing is that we can do something about this misfortune that has befallen us. We can clear these miserable memories out of our minds. We can become free of the hazard of being constantly upset by the misdirections we receive from our own minds due to the guilty feeling that has never been sensibly faced and resolved.

Rethinking our lives is perfectly possible, and is a process that can bring release from hurts that have rankled for years. We can come to know ourselves better and better by becoming detached from the troubles of the past. We can do what is seldom done in this age of demands and pressures. We can take the trouble to resee as adults what we were not given a chance to understand as children.

CHAPTER VI

CONTROLLING ANXIETIES

It would hardly be useful to ask people to let useless anxieties go if we had not discussed the problem of false guilt. For the latter very uncomfortable habit that spooks so many of us is entangled with chronic anxieties to the point where it clouds the thinking of a great many people.

Why Hang onto Inappropriate Reactions?
To a large degree we can declare that our recurrent sensations of guilt are the breeding ground of those particular anxieties that plague us continually while still remaining vague and evasive in form. The feeling of being out of sorts without good reason, of finding ourselves pushed into snapping irritably at family members or business associates with no idea of why we do so, these impulses are in general caused by irrational reasons. They come from fears taken on way back in past experience. They have no actual connection with the present, except for a relevant reminder which pushes the button to bring into memory some old, distressing occurrence that was involved with a sense of guilt.

Until we are practiced in tracing an anxiety discomfort that shows no true relationship to the present, it is wise to meet it with a generalized attitude: a reaching for belief in the possibility that we can free our minds from the habit of allowing the past to invade the present in ways that prevent us from feeling and acting like the adults we are. However, too great a struggle to discover a past connection in an unjustified fear or irritability mood is apt to bring about disappointment at a first try, if we try too hard. We can just dislodge the unpleasant mood with some such thought as: "Probably some old sense of guilt from way back is hanging around."

And we must do our best to relax. Tension is the arch inducer of poor functioning in the body or in the mind. If we want to be well, we can't give up mastering relaxation. It's just a habit, and habits can be built by priming the will with a strong "I-Want" image.

Success with relaxation in any attempt to trace causes of tension should be a preliminary to an invitation to the mind to help us. Whether seeking that name we can't recall to discovering whether we are blocked mentally because of some past misdeed, relaxing will help. Trying it first in the less important problems can begin to show what it can do in regard to clearing away false guilt influences from the subconscious mind. We should not become secretly top-lofty and sneer at this simple method, behind our hand, as it were. If we do, our subconscious mind — our one ally in finding and discarding false guilt — will drop us without a qualm. It has its own natural responses and cannot be fooled. We must be in earnest.

When we know the specific reason an anxiety mood takes over sovereignty of our minds, and builds tension in our bodies, we can deal with it. We can face it down and get rid of it by deciding whether in an alleged "act of guilt" we were truly guilty, or were we merely "supposed to be" on the basis of someone else's judgment.

It is also important to review instances in which we feel it is fair to say that we were guilty. But it is dangerous to health to hoard a sense of guilt. We can wipe out the threat of living our lives with such pile-ups if we ask ourselves, "Would I do it again?" and can give a sincere answer of "No." Even if the accusations were fair in themselves, the chances are that ninety percent of them were more parent or associate annoyance than serious child guilt.

There is very little doubt that fear is at the bottom of most of our really bitter experiences. Offhand, one might assume that rage is the true villain in life's tragedies, but it is almost exclusively a follower, not a forerunner, of fear, except in the case of what we mean by righteous indignation. For righteous indignation comes when rage is protecting love. In the same way it does in following fear, it backs up the emotion of love whether involved with a person or a belief, by expressing its protective tenderness under the guise of the force of anger.

Rage, then, is the defense the human subconscious summons to protect the threatened individual. It follows with great speed upon the advent of fear, as the means that will subdue or obliterate the cause of anxiety.

There is no essential difference between the fear-ridden conduct of a scholastic wizard and that of a jungle savage, except that with the scholastically trained person certain factors in his education act as antidotes for the fears by which he has been visited. Knowledge can do a great deal to lessen fear. What is greatly needed, though, is a habit of automatic self-command when fear strikes.

"Familiarity breeds contempt" is a genuine truth. The unknown figures frequently in the whole gamut of our experiences of fear. What we know, no matter how distasteful or frightening, has less power to paralyze our capacities than something the nature of whose threat is not familiar to us. This universal reaction of fear calling upon rage as protection is linked to the fact that the rudimentary intelligence of instinct recognizes the great disadvantage there is in unpreparedness. Where there is no reassurance from familiarity, fear is greatly increased.

We cannot, of course, be totally aware ahead of time what sorts of threat we are to be faced with, but we can act against fear of any sort by draining off its effects after an experience of intense dread. The focus on over-concern will change more rapidly if we abolish the tension of a fear-habit. It is the pile-up of old fears on new that intensifies them to the point where they interfere with present experience.

A Natural Urge Impeded by Neurosis

Fortunately for us, there is a natural urge in the body itself to let the fear go after the ordeal is over. But if neurosis is involved in a person's life a type of tenacity in the fear reaction, from anxiety experiences he has not resolved emotionally, comes into play; and it is this that too often prevents the normal instinct from letting the fear wear off in a natural way. Thus a habit of being in a state of fear can develop.

A study of contrasting instances of courage and anxiety reveals that men are not brave as automatons. Fortitude springs from thought, constructively bent on discovering advantageous points at which to take hold of a situation. Timid people, being over-concerned with negatives, make a situation insurmountable by believing it is. In the mental process of apprehension we look ahead, at times almost presciently. There is prophetic perception in this pregnant anticipation. For fear can be a seer, a clairvoyant knower of the future, when logical thought assists. Were we unable to consider, we would be forced to live like grasshoppers, eating at the moment what that moment provided. Life becomes a dungeon, however, if this great gift of foreseeing is made destructive so that we only anticipate disaster.

Hans Christian Andersen was tortured by unreasoning apprehension. He had a horror of sickness, due not so much to natural timidity as to imagination's exaggerations. A cat scratch meant he would have hydrophobia. A pain in his neck made him think he had swallowed a nail. If he had a bump on the knee, he feared dropsy. A pimple above the eye suggested blindness. R. Nisbet Bain says, "A doctor who knew him very intimately in his later years tells us how he one day met Andersen trembling all over with anxiety simply because a friend with whom he was about to make an excursion happened to arrive half an hour late.

"What he endured during that half-hour no tongue but Andersen's could ever tell. He was quite certain his friend must have come to a violent end, been run over, perhaps smashed in a collision or blown up by an explosion; and he pictured him expiring amidst the most unspeakable torments. His mind's eye had actually even seen the corpse carried home on a stretcher, all crushed and bleeding.

"He would have escaped from the horrifying sight but could not. His feet seemed rooted to the spot. He was obliged to stay and see the body of his dead friend put in a decent coffin and consigned to its last resting place. Then he pictured himself sitting down with streaming eyes, writing letters of condolence to the sorrowing relatives — and at that very moment, who should come up with smiling face and outstretched arms but the very friend whose death he had so vividly realized, and who on perceiving poor Andersen's terrible state of agitation was not only abject in his apologies, but registered a mental oath never to keep him waiting again."

There is no force within man that does not act as his

friend or foe, for the law of positive and negative expression is one of the most striking facts of consciousness. Of them all, few are more effective than the imagination as it relates to fear. We are made or unmade by this endowment, according to whether it is in command of or controlled by apprehension. A person can train himself to the place where his visual imagery is used to arouse and guide courageous action, but if fear intrudes on his visualizing power the neurotic habit will torment him.

Education Fails To Train Imagination

It is hard to understand why classical education scarcely acknowledges the importance of training the imagination. People generally, it would seem, believe it a vague and unimportant mental quality, more attributal to the impractical and slightly contemptible field of poetry than an ever-present, active agent working its will on every man in the street. We have elaborate systems of restraint to keep order in the streets, but we allow our emotions and mental functions to riot at will, then wonder why there is disquiet in our inner lives. We have not yet come to the full realization that if our inner powers were sent contentedly about their allotted tasks, we might be able to escape that terrible tightening up that makes us feel helpless.

For the sake of clarification it may be well to list the more common ways that fear works within us:

1. Imaginary, not actual, factors are always brought into the situation.

2. Improbable bogeys are invoked on the assumption that they could be there.

3. There is angry excitement, as if we sought to scare the fear away by threat.

4. Refusal of a practical solution is the rule, because such a solution does not protect against all possible dangers.

5. There tends to be a switch of focus; that is, as soon as one aspect of a fear is met, the person centers with equal anxiety upon another.

6. We spend our time trying to correct the effects of fear rather than the causes; baling the boat instead of finding the leak.

7. We tend to ignore helpful probabilities and concentrate nervously on negative possibilities.

8. In all fear, actual or imaginary, we are powerless only because of past fear images and delusional systems previously formed in the depths of consciousness.

9. The delusion of merited punishment is a common cause of torpor when one is overcome by fear.

10. We tend to rush hysterically from one wild conclusion to another, as if many answers were necessary to a single problem.

To sum up, we need to have greater understanding of fear and respect for it: respect in the sense that as caution it is invaluable to us; as terror it is a menace. And our greatest need in regard to this valuable emotion is to stop invoking it for insignificant and useless anxieties and save it for use in all legitimate threats. The emotions can be temporarily worn out, you know, from overwork.

To prevent the crystalizing of fear into a habit, at the first opportunity after experiencing anxiety of any considerable degree a person should banish the stubborn echoes of fear with specific action. He should move his arms and legs, loosening and easing them. He should bend his spine, or do any other thing that appeals to him and will move him toward complete physical relaxation. In other words, he would be expelling the natural tightness of fear by a completely relaxed body.

The great tenacity of habit once established has immense benefits for human beings. For that very reason we need to watch the development of our habits, and weed out any negative ones so that their tenacity cannot act long enough to become fixated. Why? Because the subconscious mind must be trained to help us, not hinder us, in our mastery of life.

As our minds are expert image-makers, we can set up a practice of using that flow of images to greater purpose. If we have been through an experience that threatened us physically, but have escaped it, we should dwell on the thought of gratitude for the escape, and refuse to review the threat itself over and over again. For that indulgence will only work toward setting the negative image more firmly in our minds so that it (and other such images) haunts our thoughts. Worst of all, it can occupy so much of our attention that healthful, helpful images are more and more prevented from entering. The person needs to establish images that compete with his fear.

The practice of quickly substituting a mental picture of interest or pleasurable anticipation, or even just conscious enjoyment of relaxation, can do remarkable things in finding out how to quiet one's fears and settle one's nerves.

If we really desire freedom from the depleting influence of emotions exhausted by neurosis, we should respect self-help and seek all commonsense methods to help ourselves. Search as we may for the valid assistance we find outside of ourselves, the central point remains that were Solomon himself to appear for breakfast one day, offering to make us second only to himself in wisdom, we should still have to offer our cooperation — to listen, to compare, to judge values, to test by logic and intuition whatever he might say. In other words, we would have to choose and then act on our choice, accept or reject.

The most interesting truth of all is that we wouldn't want it any other way. Our passion for personal liberty rests right there. Even children sense this deep desire to command one's own life, though they are not able to formulate mentally the ways to train the emotions with the help of the mind. It is fortunate for us and for life that we desire most definitely to be ourselves, and to be something special, as far as we are able.

This eagerness to command our own lives is sometimes called ambition, and is abused. It turns into vanity, and makes us silly. It plumps for power over others, and from time to time creates a Hitler. On the other hand, it results in magnificent minds, in helping jobs be done with incredible patience. It inspires honest action in spite of insidious temptations; and here and there large numbers of people turn up who have charm, reliability, perspective, and that essential capacity for welding humanity— humor.

In neurosis, however, there is always a fear of life built over a doubt of self. When a neurotic person is constantly plagued with undue fear, he has regressed to the spooky obsessions of a childhood world. Terrors from the primitive subconscious symbolically substitute for real trouble. Darkness seems as danger-ridden as a primeval jungle, typifying the threat of death. The sense of physicial helplessness in the dark is magnified to the point where it creates unnecessary awkwardness. Fear of the loss of love can also start panic, in which the individual loses his normal attraction as an object of love. He becomes wooden, and a false coldness engulfs him.

The lack of an adequate knowledge of intelligent methods for the handling of emotion led our ancestors to develop attitudes that in the large prevented getting command of fear. What they considered good methods of training children was in scores of ways made up of the fabric of dread. Admonitions, many of them to bend children to their will, were poured into a child's mind. They took up lodging there more and more, and so occupied his thought with the anticipation of trouble that he had difficulty giving attention to the counsel of reason. Under the weight of this mistake, apprehension became a self-inhibitory device measurably reducing the natural initiative of a normal child.

Few fears are more troublesome than the dread of self. And it is especially true when unnecessary and unfair accusations have repeatedly suggested to the defenseless subconscious of a child that he is constantly wrong in what he does or thinks.

The timesaving method of training children by force instead of reason loads them with what we might call "artificial" fear. For what it mostly succeeds in doing is to fill their minds with habits of "reading" fear into every new situation requiring decision that comes along. And the natural result is to give them a nagging uncertainty about facing new situations, along with about the worst factor in neurosis, which is conflict between thought and feeling. Fortunately for life, the nature of the life force prods children toward initiative and experimentation. But the more severe the fear of punishment, the more easily it puts a brake on natural initiative, and conflict ensues.

It is this problem that makes it so important to improve our understanding of the principles of child training, especially in regard to when, how, and why punishment should be used. The greatest need, if we wish our youngsters to grow fully mature, free of neurosis and open to happiness, is to impose a law upon ourselves; that is, to explain why correction is needed. Reasonably regular short sessions of explanation of the whys of a parent's angry reactions to a child's frustrating errors can have a value to him as great as setting up a savings account in his name. We should treat the budding intelligence with respect. It is there and can respond to reasonable explanations.

All Punishment Should Be Explained

Physical punishment induces antisocial reactions in most natures, if it is used exclusively in place of reasoning.

If an individual is ever going to be intelligent, he will be intelligent as a child — on a simpler basis, of course, than an adult who has gone through formal training. But if the child's native intelligence has never been called upon, but he is slapped or beaten or deprived with no better explanation than unsubstantiated threat delivered in a violent manner, his mind will be dangerously diverted by the instinct of self-preservation to some method of saving himself from pain and shame. And that method can be resistance — a ruse, a lie, a battle — and the opportunity to appeal to his intelligence is lost.

Penalties, of course, are a natural accompaniment to wise correction, but the unexplained blow has too much power to build neurosis to be considered a really effective step on the way to civilization. It should be reserved for crisic situations only, and intelligently explained afterward. How can we be so backward as to expect a child, untried in the innumerable consequences of thoughtless action, to anticipate such consequences and thus be able to avoid them? He has to be given a sane, quiet picture that he is interfering in other people's rights, and the fact pointed out that he is plenty demanding as to his own rights and wants.

Evil is in need of being more precisely comprehended in this scientific age. It has been given little chance to be understood for what intelligence knows it to be. Evil is ignorant or willful action against life. Sin is absence of right aim.

We should not waste valuable time bemoaning the misconceptions of our ancestors and the mishandling of education they brought about. We cannot even accuse them of intended misdeeds. Their mistakes were natural enough, given the strange mishap of evolution taking a wrong turn: when man chose to reverence intellect and school it, but backed off from trying to understand emotion and merely punished it when it caused trouble.

Now is our chance to rectify this age-old matter. We can begin to reverence more fully and wisely the great dynamic power of human emotion. But we should take the trouble to see into it as the power it is, and set our sights to enjoy its riches by understanding its gamut of reactions; and then train them so that they do not wreck our effort to build a way of life that all of us can constantly improve, protect, and enjoy.

One futile concept that has held its own in popularity since the first man stood upright is that we can win battles in human relations by ugly conduct. We may force a truce, but never do we gain the victory that is the only one that will correct the difficulty — a change of attitude in the offending person. As long as we continue to ignore the basic responses of basic emotions we shall miss our chance to make life livable.

A change of attitude can be induced, not forced. Force creates force, or retreat, not a change of mind. This foolish error of pushing the power of emotion backward instead of inviting it forward has consistently slowed down human progress. No one can expect anyone to succeed in every single instance of applying this principle. But we can say that each time we fail to use it we must resign ourselves to failure, and try again another time.

We may seem to get places by revolution. Actually we get nowhere except by evolution. The seeming success of effecting changes by revolution comes from whatever truth was presented during the revolution that changed ignorant attitudes. The misused hate, the carnage, the slaughter, are all a sad, sad waste. The true fact of this is that no individual can be forced to change an attitude. The human mind doesn't work that way. When a person sees a value he will change his mind, that is, when he really sees it; but if he is being clubbed into it, he is not apt to be willing to look.

Success with any method to get free of tyranny of

negative emotion comes from one central principle: to despise the neurotic habit. This is a use of the power and energy of rage. Obviously, it must be directed against neurotic habits, not against one's own personality, or anyone else's. This may sound like a demand for the impossible. "One has the habit. It is what is sure to happen," we say to ourselves. And that is exactly where the method needs to be applied, for this statement is untrue.

Any technique dealing with lack of emotional adjustment is usually required to be a dual process: against or for. It is necessary always to hate a crippling habit that is making life harder than it should be. But as we summon the emotional energy of rage to repudiate a bad habit, we must reassure the sense of self. This requires normal respect and regard for the self. It is possible to have a well-balanced sense of esteem for our own nature. It is in fact essential to the rooting out of any feeling of inferiority and that bane of intelligent self-estimation — false guilt.

Cooperation from the Subconscious

There is another essential factor in the value to us of using specific methods to clear embarrassing neurotic habits out of our common experience. It is the fact that we must accept the nature of the human subconscious, and determine to win it over in the game of "which is going to boss us": the positive powers and abilities of our natures, or the duplicity and rapacity the subconscious can display if we let it.

We must keep in mind that the subconscious mind is obedient. It does without question what the conscious and superconscious (the spirit) of a person tells it is wanted. But it is the source of emotional power per se; and that means it can support a noble life, or , if allowed, put into practice the dregs of the four emotions and produce monsters of cruelty, cowardice, lust, or spite.

If we really desire to be a person with the kind of self-command and knowledge that spell success in the broadest sense, we must communicate constructively with the powerplant of our nature — the subconscious area of our mind. Power is there and can waste away in semi-idleness, or worse, if our ability to choose is slouching through life with no worthwhile purpose and no vivid images to stimulate the will.

We are gradually becoming aware that we have assets of power and ability that we have only half, or less, understood. Therefore, we have received only a portion of the benefit of their assistance. For example, we should not seek to obliterate fear entirely. By so doing we would lose one of our greatest powers. As with courage, the higher expression of rage, we need to value fear because it can be turned into caution, discretion, and consideration. Also by fearing to offend love we can develop that open sesame of human communication — kindness.

CHAPTER VII

HIDDEN CAPACITIES

Is Common Sense Always Sensible?

The homespun idea of common sense is shrewder than it seems, for when it truly is common sense, a simple inner realization of an aspect of practical truth, it is worth noticing. It is also important to know how to be sure that common sense is sensible before we become tricked by its failure to be so.

Many a witticism has been helpful in the effort of the human race to discover truth. Van Wyck Brooks indicated most aptly the befuddlement human beings can display when they are tripped up by the pompous self-deceptions embedded in the neurosis. In *A Writer's Notebook*, Brooks said that "earnest people are often people who habitually look on the serious side of things that have no serious side," and revealed how common it is to leave out the "sense" in what we call common sense.

With science having brought a brand-new demand for precision into life, we are faced with the need to produce an equivalent, if not a duplicate way of dealing with the realm of thought and feeling, which cannot be reached completely by methods that readily apply to material things.

In the development of common sense the race has

been groping for the assurances of truth, and not too infrequently succeeding in hitting the nail on the head, or at least pushing it part way into the wood. But since the development of common sense in our outlook on experience springs mainly from subconscious sources, and is always subject to neurotic ways of reacting to things, it could be of some help to us to look a little harder at our common attitudes. And there is little doubt that the one area of human response that should have our best attention is the powerplant of the emotions. They have been allowed too much opportunity to air their immense force in anything but winsome ways.

There is great need in average life for average people to notice the way they allow too much feeling to attach itself to ordinary, far from cataclysmic occurrences. Take afterthoughts for example. We would save ourselves a lot of misery if we would spare ourselves the distress that comes with these nags that so often haunt us in estimating something we have done or said as perhaps not the very best way to have done it or said it.

"Did I make a fool of myself?" our egos shudder. "Did I put my foot in it with Bill about that contract?" So what? If, when we next meet Bill we are relaxed, good-humored, and free of nervousness, if he hasn't forgotten the matter altogether he will do so then and there. We are much too apt to lug a heavy load of what we have decided were awkward actions or comments along with us from the past. And then we compound the error by tightening up the next time, and doing maybe even worse. It isn't common sense to allow one's present responses to be distorted by past experience.

A client burst into my office one day looking like the small boy who has just thought up the greatest plan of all time.

"What happened to you?" I asked.

"I've developed a method of my own to stop worrying

about making mistakes."

"Fine," I encouraged him. "What is it?"

"It's called 'The hell, it's done' technique," he beamed. "If I'm afraid I've made a bad boner — or even if I'm sure I have — I say to myself, 'Aw, hell, it's done.' I think out how it should have been handled, give myself absolution, and start fresh. I've already been through a couple of incidents where it worked. I just decided I'd do better next time, and pushed the whole thing out of my mind." He paused, and then murmured to himself, "It's amazing how it works."

"It will," I said emphatically. "If we will give our mind orders, often enough and distinctly enough, it will set up methods that will bring about the results we want."

That is a truth, not an infantile vagary. It is a known, successfully practiced technique to use the obedience of our subconscious mind to correct troublesome habits. It is the essence of common sense to discover and use methods to be found in our own mind, to relieve us of embarrassing tricks we have inadvertently picked up. It should be done in an easy, quiet, relaxed way. And it must be repeated.

In this exciting age of discovery it would be foolish to let technology run off with the laurels. There may be laurels enough to go around for every one of us if we will open the mental doors that lead to the needed knowledge. And we shouldn't forget that the majority of troublesome emotional habits were formed when we were very young, and that therefore, to start with, a very simple method to correct a bad habit is the only thing consistent with our thought and mood when the habit was formed. We are fools if we are afraid to try to free ourselves from emotional bondage.

The man with the homemade technique worked out some proof of the fact that allowing himself to be nervous and tense when he was faced with something requiring his best abilities, reduced those abilities to a pitiful mockery of his true capacity. He also told me that he suspected he met such instances with subconscious resentment over the criticism he anticipated, and consequently with resistance. So how could he escape the tension that caused the boners? Subconscious resentment is a powerful parent of subconscious resistance.

So we see that common sense is not quite as common as the well-worn phrase implies.

Standing Still Blocks Evolution

We can't stand still, physically and mentally, and keep evolution going. When we do it is perhaps the reason we are at last shoved into revolution, when by serving evolution with our best attention we could roll smoothly forward by means of the more benign process it provides. Revolution has become the most expensive means for the growth of man into civilization. Obviously we can no longer afford it. What we need to do is to look more sharply at what evolution offers us, and incorporate our findings into instruction that is truly educational, not just informational.

It is weird how we can clutch and cling to some miniscule slight or rudeness when it is a prime method for offering the advantage to the enemy on a silver platter. We dwell on such a happening with morbid relish, as though it were the latest highly advertised candy bar; and are too busy concentrating on this subhuman indulgence to move into a mood with the power to set the situation straight.

If paid attention to, inconsequential, though unpleasant happenings in experience constitute a dragging weight that, among other symptoms, can bring the common cold down upon us with unnecessary frequency. And why? Because in spite of the overall toughness and well-nigh

miraculous recuperative power of the human organism
it is also delicate, suggestible, and capable of being
"thrown" by the mismanagement of our endowment of
emotion.

Inadequately educated as we still are in the significance
of the hidden forces of human life, we allow resistance
to build up in our feeling area over an incredible number
of inane, superficial experiences. But where can we go
to get understandable information in regard to this truly
vital factor of life? Sources are developing, but we should
avoid departmentalizing the knowledge we need by
the kind of formal language that so separates people
from common life. Life gets vitality from common speech,
and thus any informational data loses much of its useful
force in the specialized atmosphere of scientific jargon.

If we wish to be healthy, happy, productive living
organisms, we must insist that the world of visible things,
including the scientific world, open its arms to the
world of the invisible. Science must honor the right of
the spiritual side of life to develop its half of the needs
that will bring our experience into balance. Such cooperation is essential to provide the ingredients necessary
for developing a delight in living.

Why is it that, though we may gape for a moment or
two at the many usable concepts that have come out of
the minds of men, we do so little to let them waken and
expand our thought and then our action? Out of the pene-
tration of Shakespeare's tremendous awareness came
the comment, "In nature there's no blemish but the
mind . . . " And we had to wait centuries for Newton
and others to start science going by stumbling on a new
"method of attention." This now creates the need for a
parallel effort to make miracles of improvement happen
in the realm of human responses that affect human relations.

Not even a Midas can endure life if he cannot attain

satisfying relationships with other human beings. There must be some lack of common sense somewhere in our handling of ourselves if we can accumulate so much gain from the visible world and yet find ourselves still struggling in a cocoon of disruptive emotional confusion and weakened beliefs.

We have little difficulty knowing whether our faces and hands are clean and our hair in or out of order. But we are not always as quick to recognize when our voices are going to come out sharply rather than agreeably, or that something is lurking at the door of the subconscious, ready to feed us fear and dull the keen edge of our efficiency. We should become familiar as eating with the habits of emotion — natural and neurotic — so that we can clear away our negatively conditioned reactions and get ourselves time and better conditions for developing the positive promise of mankind's emotional wealth.

We have some catching up to do with understanding mental ability as contrasted with emotional power, and how to relate the two to build our lives on a sounder basis. By now it seems evident that merely training the intellect and setting it up as the central goal in view was a most dangerous venture, tempting as it no doubt was. But our emotions far surpass our intellects in power to disrupt life if they are not trained to understand life cooperatively. To start such training we should become much better acquainted with one particular word and what it means to us all. That word is "cause," and it is nothing less than the arbiter, the be-all and end-all of our lives.

A Special Aspect of Good Sense

Never was there a time when it would be more the essence of good sense for us to achieve a simple, workable understanding of the place cause inhabits in life and its ever-present, endless, potent influence upon us. Francis Bacon said, "To know truly is to know by causes," and Voltaire went so far as to express his belief that "chance is a word void of sense; nothing can exist without a cause."

This is not to imply that cause and effect, as a constant condition in our experience, is unknown to average people. It is merely to suggest that we think of it too casually as a scholarly idea, somewhat removed from common experience, when the truth is we should be approaching it as an experience common indeed. It is not being given the heed it needs, to help us protect ourselves from flouting cause by our impudent neglect of it and thus falling into a welter of mismatched effects.

Facility in relating cause and effect in our minds from day to day should be as common an experience as adding figures to balance our books, or estimating costs and expenditures to avoid getting into debt. This omnipresent relationship between what produces everything we experience and the factors resulting therefrom should be searched for in the invisible world of feeling much more ardently that it has been. Until we do this it will be sheer naivete to believe we can attain stability in human relations.

Causes, when found, may not always edify our egos, but admitting them, if only in the secrecy of our minds, is a vital step in removing much danger from life. For unkempt emotions are the guilty parties in a high percentage of our troubles. And emotions become unkempt when we ignore the causes that start them off into tantrums.

Let's Start Refining Our Crude Forces

It is becoming clear that self-respect, which humanity, in spite of its confused concepts, does apparently value, should include more acute respect for our power to refine our crude forces. Thus murderous desires could become a thing of the past, terror be close to unknown, lust better balanced with generous affection, and spiteful inquisitiveness be supplanted by legitimate interest.

We have been endowed by the Creator with incredible strengths that need study, guidance, and appreciation if we are not to be swamped by their power. Intellectuality will not do it, because the basic function of human power is emotion, and acumen is very nearly helpless in its overexpressed presence. If we expect to subdue this pristine force so that life is safe for men, women, and children, we shall have to fight fire with fire. We shall have to long for the peace and safety to be gained by having our emotions at our own command. We shall have to value these emotions enough to teach ourselves the great central protection of self-command, so that we can live with them, perfect them, and enjoy them forever.

So, to handle the problem of the increasing emotional disturbances in life we need to learn to take command of the cause of negative emotions, which often does not stop to gild the lily or hesitate and stammer as to its own wishes. It can be subdued only by a concerted effort of the human galaxy of gifts which cluster around the two great impulses of wisdom and love. It's time we began to stand a little in awe of the nascent power contained in our own natures and of the Power which bestowed the gift and its endless promise. We need to take some thought of how emotion can be induced to accept direction from the human spirit — the center and designer of all positive human impulse.

THE BASIC TECHNIQUE

Command of Attention:
To change a habit of over-emotional reaction to someone's unpleasant, callous, untrue, or threatening action

or remark, we don't wait for either rage or self-pity to take command of our thought. We project our thought instantly into a consideration of the other person's thought. What is his or her possible feeling at the time: positive or negative? Is it justified? Is it not perhaps the result of negative conditioning in the other person's life, possibly a repetition of unpleasant, callous, untrue or threatening actions or remarks in his own past? Our reactive impulse can be changed from negative to positive by this break into average reflex action, and can be retoned for a sensible response.

Now, this may sound like an abject giving in to abuse. But considering the sorry-go-round factor of the negative conditioning of sensitive youthful feelings so common in life experience, would it not be worth experimenting with our own reactions to see if the weary repetition of this unfortunate life process couldn't be broken, at least in one instance, on one occasion, to see what happened?

There are almost endless reasons why such a confrontation may have come about, each one offering a plausible explanation for the difficulty. But this one act of substituting the quick response of a fortified attitude of understanding can revolutionize human relations. It can break the too frequent inadvertent mistake of acting on the negative conditioning from the early life of the offending party. If this method works, it can inspire the intended victim with a gleeful sense of victory in taking a shot at the ball and chain of repetitive negative response.

Incidentally, our ability to do this against the long list of time-honored reasons for not doing it is a triumph in itself. It is no small accomplishment to catch our own angry response before it puts a fresh link in the negative reflex action chain. We have to start somewhere, sometime, to improve our response habits, to remove them from the area of reflex action and gain the power to say what, how, when, or whether they shall be the same old clanking chain, or evidence of an individual in charge of his or her attention and in command of the realm of feeling.

This type of experiment can rescue us from the painful habit of exposing ourself as a target for something we should have never paid attention to in the first place. And it starts to train our power of choice in deciding to ignore false, unfair, or malicious accusation or suggestion.

Why not be satisfied with depriving the other person of success in pushing us into emotional violence and distress?

Mercy Begins At Home

In sheer mercy for others in any difficulties with them, we should give a thought or two to the rough going they may have had as children, even in a good home, so-called. If there was lack in those simple explanations of their obligation to learn the art of sane living, they will be virtually compelled into belligerent reflex action by habit.

Until we accept the fact that the ego is not the full personality but a conditioned representation of the identity, we shall probably have to wait too long for the lion to lie down with the lamb. It demands an informed identity sense to be willing to show the mercy suggested above. And it cannot attain the end in view on the right occasion unless the person from whom it is required has thought about the matter and knows how to balance mercy (love) with intelligence (wisdom). For love can be too soft without wisdom; and wisdom can be too impersonally hard without kindness.

This sort of "action in balance" produces the kind of common sense that can bring about practical results. If a husband has accepted the common sense of at least trying to consider his wife's "battle of the ego," and mercifully allows that knowledge to dictate terms to him in any battle in the marital state, we have a sample of evolution saving an otherwise destructive situation that could unnecessarily end a marriage. And if the wife can meet this pristine generosity with a parallel offer, we have the beginning of a process that would lead to peace on earth. Could the sop of the gift of a mink stole really exceed in value the uniting of two generous purposes?

But to get any reliable results in stabilizing the relation of the sexes, we shall have to study how greatly the false face of the acquired ego features can distort the basic potentials of the true self. Haphazard training of the young can perpetuate the primitive expression of the emotions, as fury, terror, lust, and invasion of the privacy of others (the misuse of wonder).

If we are really sincere in our desire to set life right by taking on the job of attempting to direct the power of our emotions instead of letting them run rampant, we should view this idea with a care that has something in it of the dedication to religion.

We have not begun to get the values out of mankind's attraction to religion. In a start toward reorganizing our attitudes toward this natural hunger to relate ourselves to the Life-Cause, of which we ourselves are primary effects, we scarcely need to go further than to say that such an urge is the acme of common sense. One can scarcely benefit fully from a Cause one has not admitted. How fortunate it is for us that the gifts keep arriving whether we condescend to admit the Cause or not.

Experts in technology have to have respect for causes: the forces that bring everything into being. They are soundly convinced that if they do not give cause constant attention they will be unable to bring about the results, the effects, they desire. Also they will release unnecessary threat into their efforts. In other words, they cannot afford tantrums when dealing with their technological endeavors. Though their materials do not scream and curse at them, they do contain powers and dangers which are seriously respected by the experimenters.

A Value To Become Acquainted With

But in spite of the radical difference between the material things we can construct and the immaterial ones we so crave, there is one law that relates to both; in either case, we must become better acquainted with, and more acceptant of, the causes that produce the effects that we want.

We can't reach out and pluck an automobile off a tree. This we have accepted. We have to wait for someone to imagine an automobile, to desire it enough to discover the necessary causal processes that will produce it, and then to build it. A similar process is necessary to stir us into attaining what we immensely wish for on the immaterial side of life: regard from others, success in daily living (with the protection to attain it), contentment about material possessions, the joys of a happy home life, and peace throughout the world.

Apropos of the latter suggested desire, do we realize fully that attaining universal peace comes up against the force of the unregenerated ego? If a person has given his adult life to perfecting himself as a fighting man and gained a position of power, the ego cannot lightly see that power taken away from him.

As it happens, none of these natural problems can be solved until everyone sees how essential it is for us to study the cause-and-effect rhythms in the realm of thought and feeling. For "the will obeys the image in the mind"; and the quantity of images dealing with power, with fighting, and with conquest, especially in the masculine world, must be understood and dealt with before we can escape eternal disorder in life.

If we did not have in our human makeup the two balancing gifts of mental and emotional reaction, we would have less ability but might escape a source of confusion in trying to make sense more common. It would have seemed common sense for the schools to have given students a vivid, less vague idea of how important cause is in our immediate lives, and what effect means in relation to it, since on this great relationship most of common experience rests. But while "cause and effect" is a common enough phrase, and appears often in print, its down-to-earth meaning for the individual has not been put often enough into phraseology that would help him understand its effect upon his own life.

One would be led to think no one ever took the trouble to learn to relate cause and effect when we observe how often someone will "fly off the handle" at a remark that to ourselves has little or no cause to offend anyone. We do not see the cause, for it is embedded in the history of the angered person's conditioning. If we knew that history intimately, we could probably pinpoint the reason for the reaction of anger with very little trouble.

This misuse of the energy rage can provide will continue its wastage until the mighty rhythm of cause and effect is ABC to every schoolchild. Or until we take on self-help's job of clearing out of our minds those perpetuated negative reactions set up in childhood and never reviewed to determine their appropriateness for an adult.

It is not so much basic rage that is such a danger. It is rage neuroticized in an individual in his youth, and never clarified or assuaged, that manifests in this overwhelming fashion. If this is so, we see how valuable individual self-help could be in returning to normal the emotions that have been driven into neurotic habits by putting too much strain on a child's ignorance, and by pushing his emotional impulses into frenzies he must suppress for fear of punishment.

The worship of technology has pushed our noses into a

plethora of enticing possibilities in the visible world, so that the invisible realm — the Source, not of our creature comforts, but of our every permanent joy — has been sadly neglected. It is the Designer of Life that has tucked away in our evolving organisms every potential for understanding ourselves and improving our lot. We must dig those potentials out, however. They lie inert until the stream of consciousness chooses, from its endless flow of images, the one that fires the higher mind (con-science) to value a given image enough to dwell on it and thus attract the will to put it into action.

Our lives are dependent upon the existence of a Creator as a life force, sustaining from day to day the existence and capacity for the very breathing of the human race. To turn ingrate to such endowment could turn out to be dangerous indeed.

Human life and human capacities exist. They are causal and their effects must come from existing sources. There can be no effect without a cause. It is the wildest misconception to deny the Cause of our own existence; for in a certain peculiarly insistent way an assumption of "no God" denies that we ourselves exist. To exist from *no* cause is an impossibility. However, it must be definitely a lack of common sense to expect, at our present level of development, to believe that we can ascertain the full nature of the existence when we are so far behind in the prodigious need of directing safely our own basic emotions.

Man in some way demonstrates his being made in the image of God by his ability to manifest partially, via the mystical sleight of hand of imagination, the creative function of Deity. But when he attempts to usurp the origin of creativity, he falls somewhat short of Divine scope. If man were willing to accept with gratitude the amazing degree of creativity that he has, and remember that he follows the Great Designer, he could succeed incredibly. He has done so to an encouraging degree already. However, it is still fairly rare, because the meanings involved are not thought about by enough people to create a concensus, in human groups and finally in the world. And the failure is too often caused by the gap in the system of education that leaves out of recognition the three basic principles of wisdom, love, and their expression in the highest forms.

The understanding of one's emotions, their power, and the danger to life if they are not made harmless and vitally productive by raising them above their primitive level, is a natural prerequisite of the hope of experiencing the best there is in living.

The shadow of the so far perennial struggle between love (woman) and wisdom (man) still nags at our chance to solve our problems. The inevitable force behind each of these two life influences can never cease. Principles do not cease, they are merely made ineffective because the false concepts of the ego interfere with man's attention to what they really mean and how great their value is.

The spirit of a life principle just cannot be safely defied or refused. It can only be preserved by deeper understanding of its guardianship of sanity, and by intelligent obedience to encouraging its growth.

Real love, in any form, is a high point in experience. Demeaning it will always end in loss.

Real wisdom is not common, and often irrationally claimed or attributed. But defying or defaming it delays the greater part of humanity's hopes.

Use — that is, fulfillments in action — can be neglected or reduced in value. If so, we languish in irrepressible confusion and frustration.

This is hardly the purpose intended in common sense. And it would be better if it did not become too common.

CHAPTER VIII

DISCOVER A GREATER YOU

Becoming Twice-Born

It is impossible to bring a person back to what we think of as normality if he has been seriously neurotic; he can only become supernormal. After fully understanding what negative conditioning can do and its relation to the ego, he is twice-born; once physically, and again to a new mental-emotional life. He makes adjustment by a means beyond the conditions and circumstances of his time. He sees things with new understanding and well conceived attitudes. The ignorance and super-stition which injured his consciousness in the past no longer have any real influence over him. He has regained the simplicity and naturalness of the child, but has in-creased his wisdom as an adult. He is again *in* life, but not *of* life. His whole mental-emotional system reacts from a different basis, with less nervousness and more strength.

Freedom from neurosis will always put a person in a better position to deal with what life brings to him. It is amazing how people waste their time, strength, safety, and peace of mind by not communicating with their own mental powerhouse. Whenever we feel rage or fear begin to bubble up within us, we should instantly enter into silent conversation with ourselves. We should put our subconscious minds through a questionnaire on the subject of whether we are justly angry or afraid.

If we will try this we can set up a habit of cutting negative feeling off before it takes over and can't be stopped. And our emotional powerhouse will gradually learn to put itself through the required questionnaire on its own. It will do it much faster, too, than our conscious mind can. So before long there will be no necessity for us to be concerned about deciding to do it. We will have set up concepts and standards as to what is not worth paying attention to.

This practice can be an exercise in self-education that can clear all sorts of foolish and childish concepts and habits out of our mind. It is a fact that certain immature ideas, started in youth, and never reviewed for their suitability in adulthood, cause wrangle after wrangle through life, and should be discarded by self-questioning. Images of quietness, good humor, fair play, patience, and the like can be planted in the lower consciousness, to do all the work and relieve us ultimately of even having to think about it. It will become automatic, although it obviously cannot be expected to do so without practice. Its satisfactory performance is built on the law of growth from performance, just as all good human habits are.

We have been admitting that the emotions are fast and powerful. But there is that area of consistency to be depended upon as expressed in the law: the will obeys the image in the mind. Also wise caution and logical persuasion can turn the puerility of haphazard rage into a controlled and useful weapon when it is actually needed. A voice that quietly means what it says can take the wrangle out of many an unnecessary altercation, and seldom fail to get a kind of attention from others that tends to end in intelligent and amicable results.

It is a burdensome thing to pile up emotional debts by ignoring or fighting the truths about emotion. The fatigue that follows most inconsequential quarrels could account for a great deal of the problem of succumbing to illness. The same is true about fear that is allowed to wander around in consciousness, gathering strength from images that coddle it when they should be supplanted by positive pictures of any and every sort until reason can reign and common sense take over the stream of consciousness.

Life so far has never been free of the battle with ignorance. But it also has never lacked man's struggle to overcome ignorance, slow and, alas, stupid at it as he has too often been. But today, much as there is to do, a direction is being taken that offers hope of release from some of the more futile ways of trying to attain more maturity, such as the attempt to throttle negative emotion and drive it back into ineptitude.

Stop Putting "Meaning" in Second Place

Now that we are aiming for understanding of all the forces we find ourselves endowed with in life, and are looking for methods of constructive direction and use of force per se, both inside and outside of ourselves, we are pointed toward greater possibilities of increasing intelligence itself. We are beginning to see that we must give up putting subjective awareness and meaning in second place, and tilting our attention on too great a slant toward objective progress and action.

James Stephens believed that "women are wiser than men because they know less and understand more." Now, before our brother man rises in scorn against such seeming defection, let's point out that it is actually a statement quite consistent with the basic natures of the two sexes. Men certainly do tend to know more, of facts and their relationships, of uses and values, and that capacity gives a pretty consistent result in intelligence. But feeling, which is where women are more basically endowed, does produce a kind of understanding that is different from intellect but very important to life. We have the term "woman's intuition," which gives women, especially, those imprecise but significant awarenesses that do not fit into the intellectual categories at which men are so adept.

It is then a fact that in general women are intuitive, and this reaction can be very valuable, especially in human relations. Wordsworth's comment that "faith becomes a passionate intuition," seems to imply a way that this feminine characteristic affects the elements of life expression. We could not live a day without rushing into confusion and hysteria if we were not capable of "practical" faith: in the flight captain, the gas stove, the alarm clock, the sun, the supermarket manager, and so on and on. It seems worthwhile also to note that the "intuitional urges" of women have drawn them rather noticeably toward a type of reality that typifies the hopes and promises of religion.

There comes a time when an interested student of the psychology of human relations gladly admits the contentiousness of his ego, and with a humorous awareness debunks his self-justifications. The sooner we learn to do this, the more rapidly we will progress in release from negative emotional pressure.

Scores of people waste the opportunity presented to them by books on humanity's troubles by criticizing and denying the points involved in an author's thought, not to speak of ignoring the hours of his experience. They debate from the angle of the affronted ego, for the sake of winning, not from any desire to learn.

Mentioning this problem does not mean that we want anybody to become credulous. We are merely too familiar with the effect of conditioning on people. It creates a difficulty about being aware of the reactive emotional habits established in us by being thrown helplessly into the youthful struggle against negative conditioning, and the powerful impulse to find our own identities. Because of the tricks neurosis plays on our thinking we need to ponder the means by which we can rid ourselves of such emotional distortions.

It is wise to list the times we are inclined to "yes, but" as we read. It is a good idea to note down just what we have been most inclined to contend. After we have collected eight or ten strong disagreements we should look them over to see if there is not a connecting and familiar thread running through them, and then turn our emotion of wonder free to react with curiosity as to what kind of conditioning we think most roused us to resistance. We may find we want to change an attitude or two.

It is also valuable to check on the way we take refuge in "facts," when the spirit and the motives involved point to important significances. Truth often lies in the connotations, the inner meanings, more than in the denotations or data. It is in the latent, not in the manifest, content of thought that one finds much of real truth.

It is no use attempting self-help as long as one fights like a Don Quixote to retain every phantom concept of neurosis. Intellectuality is never intelligent until it admits the great simplicities in the realities of life. We can argue ourselves clear out of the human scene by showing off our erudition rather than looking honestly for basic truths.

If a person is in genuine earnest about his mental health, it is wise, often essential, to separate himself occasionally from the too familiar habits of activity. It is doubtful if anyone can get very far in freeing himself from neurosis if he is afraid or unwilling to face his own thoughts, and interpret his difficulties.

Jesus went into the wilderness for forty days of meditation. Buddha meditated regularly. They would have looked with scorn at the hurried superficiality of the average American who tries the therapeutic methods of psychology. Socrates bored patiently below the surface of human thought into the centers of feeling and of belief. He was passionate about experiencing truth.

All Significant Men Contemplate

Our own leaders were known to give themselves to extended times of prayerful quiet. Lincoln grew in moral structure through a habit of profound contemplation. Emerson and Thoreau got help from nature. Every thinker worthy of the name has had times of separating himself from the clack and clash of existence to seek the deeper inspiration he believed necessary to a safe and sound way of life.

Such men believed in pursuing spiritual knowledge. They gave time to it. Giving time to psychical growth is an essential step in therapeutic change. A person should safeguard sincerity by a deliberate appointment with his identity. No matter how busy our life, with business problems confusing us or half a dozen children climbing into our lap, we can secure a moment now and then during which to evaluate life and its truths. If we use this oasis of peace for worry, it will become valueless. It must be for personal communion with positive concepts. A ritual, a farce, is all that remains if we do not keep faith with the possibility of changing our egos back into our identities.

That is why we must persistently exclude the nervous details which clamor to crowd into this space of pressureless calm. All we forgot to do, all we fear may happen, the trials and tribulations of our whole life come stalking into this sanctum we have dared to set up. If we do not drive such specters out, no matter what their insistence, we doom utterly any worthwhile result. We must grow in awareness of the possibilities embedded in life.

Such contemplation is essential to producing spiritual transitions. Until we give up hating those who hurt us, we retain our hypersensitivity. Until we cease to be arrogant, pride denies us forgiveness and compassion. Unless we come to care for interior and eternal growth, petty patterns of success will engender feelings of inferiority, or unfounded superiority.

Such a choice requires singleness of purpose. Distractions and the uproar of life must be evaded. To return again and again to the simple task of putting the tumult away is the very core of psychological release. It must be always followed by a real formation of the image of change which the heart is seeking. Cure cannot come unless we have seen it first clearly in the mind's eye.

Worship is vital to growth and to health. How many people think about it as a vitalizing of the human spirit? Love moves mountains. Without its energy, wisdom is powerless and nothing of true satisfaction is ever realized. We must long for the progress we are intellectually considering. We change when we love the newer ways. Success follows the leading of a passion of interest.

Also, we owe it to ourselves and to life to exercise gratitude. If we choose one thing for which we are grateful, think about it, and impress it deeply upon our attention, we are inviting health into our bodies by expressing this attitude of health in our minds.

We have been hearing a great deal about affirmation. A whole new school of philosophy, even religion, is growing up around this recognition. Why? For a very significant reason: It has power. The factor of life's response to affirmation is one of the mysteries of experience, and one of the greatest of all promises. The truth is, we don't know why it works; we just know it does. We don't know what electricity is or how it does what it does. We light our houses with it, run our equipment, and do many things too numerous to list.

Bravery, courage, the adventure spirit, curiosity, wonder, and enthusiasm are affirmative powers. We see them produce amazing results before our eyes. Each, we must assume, has its own dynamic potential. Thus each, we must assume, is capable of producing a responsive channel for its expression. Of course each uses mental images for producing results, and the image has its own propulsive power.

The point is that we know the human qualities of courage, enthusiasm, reverence, and faith have power not too different from electricity. They have not been explored or exploited to the degree that electricity has, but they have announced their usefulness to man and he is beginning to make a better and better use of them. They are the dynamos in the "science of satisfaction," and can lead us out of our present manifold problems.

The backbone of the affirmative attitude is constructive anticipation. It keeps the mind open. When the mind is open it comprehends more fully and more quickly. Constructive anticipation is a searching process. The mind is organized for a hunt. The great researchers float along on the tide of constructive anticipation; they work hard but seldom think of it as labor because the effect of constructive anticipation is to keep interest so alive that the work does not seem arduous.

Were doubt to enter this state of constructive anticipation, the burden of the work would immediately become apparent. Fatigue would enter to a serious degree. The skeptic scorns affirmation. He closes his mind to discovery. He usually muddles around endlessly in critical analysis of what already is, closing the door to the discoveries that might make life more palatable to him.

The Great "Listener"

Knowing as we now do that everybody's subconscious mind is a great "listener," and that repetition finally attracts subconscious attention to the support of a given image, we can't plead ignorance as an excuse to ignore the fact. It's too important. And we cannot evade the truth that we should avoid any negative thoughts that will compel the area of adverse emotional force to act, turning constructive images into negative ones. For that would put us at a disadvantage, in health and happiness, and offer emotionally toxic suggestions to our associates.

What we need for a better life are individuals solidly in command of their own minds, and enthralled with the game of setting life straight by setting straight their own imagery and thus making their wills into engines for the regeneration of life.

The necessary act of balancing the power of the identity with the influence of constructive humility is a delicate one. We need to learn how to give this strong, instinctive awareness of self adequate leeway to offer uncompromised help, both to itself and to others. To make the distinctions to gain this balance between the rights and needs of the self and those of the neighbor is no mean task. It might almost be called the greatest issue we face. And the signs indicate that winning this victory has much to do with the survival of the race.

The prime reason why it pays to become acquainted with the laws of the universe is because nothing is successful that goes against them. On the physical plane this is very obvious. You cannot step out of a tenth story window and walk away from the scene. Fire will destroy your flesh. Even man-made law will not permit you willfully to hold your head under water for an hour. They call it suicide.

There are equivalent situations in the realm of thought and feeling, with the same simple but devastating relation to cause and effect. Try the experiment of screaming an accusation at someone you dearly love. There will be shocked consternation and an immediate resentful response, even if only a glance. The nerves of the human organism react along certain definite lines. They telegraph messages to the brain that bring responses consistent with the stimulus. It is a law, and laws are orderly.

We have tried to bypass this unalterable fact that action and reaction are equal, or we have wasted precious time sputtering and inveigling against it. But this truth is hard to take only because of our resistance to any blockage of our egos. As a matter of fact, such laws work for our ultimate satisfaction, not every little whim that flits through our heads.

Neurosis is no more a problem than life itself is a job to be learned before we can become expert at it. Understanding its needs and purposes is a required course for being alive. We are, as it were, just waking up to the miracle of Creation, and realizing that we must reevaluate ourselves as the main exemplars of that immense event. We must discover how to prevent that type of mental-emotional stalemate that caused so many of the ancient attempts at civilization to miscarry. They seemed never able to discover fully what balance is, what purpose it serves, the way in which it holds the contrasting elements of life together. They were not aware of the danger of allowing either of the two vast aspects of objective and subjective realities, the visible and invisible elements of existence, to supersede the other.

Yet it is so plain to see that "all objects and no meanings" ends in a surfeit of superfluous things and empty actions; while meanings, which serve the spirit, cannot alone supply man's objective necessities. If these two essential needs of human life can be brought into better balance by acceptance of their individual importance, the value of each will be increased and their combined contributions to life strengthened to the point of making a stable civilization possible.